Polyunsaturated Cooking

Beth Cockburn-Smith

CHARTWELL
BOOKS INC.

Acknowledgements

The author and publisher would like to thank the following
for their help in sponsoring photographs for this book:
Birds Eye Foods Limited   pages 31 and 55
Buxted Advisory Service   pages 86–87
Charbonnier Wines   pages 34–35
Colman's Mustard   pages 78–79
Dexham International   pages 42–43
Flora Information Service   pages 71 and 74–75
Knorr   pages 18–19
Mazola Pure Corn Oil   pages 23, 26–27, 58–59 and 63
Mushroom Growers' Association   pages 10–11
New Zealand Lamb Information Bureau   page 91
Olives from Spain   page 47
Pasta Foods Limited   page 15
Sharwoods Limited   pages 50–51
Veuve du Vernay   page 83

Photograph on page 39 by Angel Studio
All other photography by Vic Paris of Alphaplus Studios,
Leatherhead
Colour illustrations by Robin Laurie
Line drawings by Ann Rees
Consultant nutritionist Jenny Salmon

Published by Chartwell Books Inc.,
A Division of Book Sales Inc.,
110 Enterprise Avenue, Secaucus, New Jersey 07094

© Copyright The Hamlyn Publishing Group Limited 1978

ISBN 0-89009-195-1
LOC Catalog Card Number 77-99167

Phototypeset in Great Britain by
Filmtype Services Limited, Scarborough
Printed in Hong Kong

Contents

Useful Facts and Figures   4

Introduction   5

Cholesterol and the Diet   6

Which Foods?   9

Starters   11

Soups   19

Fish   27

Meat   35

Poultry and Game   43

Vegetable Dishes and Salads   51

Sauces and Basic Recipes   59

Just Desserts   67

Cakes and Biscuits   75

Special Occasions   79

Buffet Parties   87

Index   94

Useful Facts and Figures

Notes on metrication

In this book quantities are given in metric, Imperial and American measures. Exact conversion from Imperial to metric measures does not usually give very convenient working quantities and so the metric measures have been rounded off into units of 25 grams.

Ounces	Approx g to nearest whole figure	Recommended conversion to nearest unit of 25
1	28	25
2	57	50
3	85	75
4	113	100
5	142	150
6	170	175
7	198	200
8	227	225
10	283	275
12	340	350
14	396	400
16 (1 lb)	454	450

Note: When converting quantities over 16 oz first add the appropriate figures in the centre column, then adjust to the nearest unit of 25. As a general guide, 1 kg (1000 g) equals 2.2 lb or about 2 lb 3 oz.

Liquid measures The millilitre has been used in this book and the following table gives a few examples.

Imperial	Approx ml to nearest whole figure	Recommended ml
$\frac{1}{4}$ pint	142	150 ml
$\frac{1}{2}$ pint	283	300 ml
1 pint	567	600 ml
$1\frac{1}{2}$ pints	851	900 ml
$1\frac{3}{4}$ pints	992	1000 ml (1 litre)

Spoon measures All spoon measures given in this book are level unless otherwise stated.

Can sizes At present, cans are marked with the exact (usually to the nearest whole number) metric equivalent of the Imperial weight of the contents, so we have followed this practice when giving can sizes.

Flour Plain flour is used in the recipes, unless specified otherwise.

Seasoned flour This is flour seasoned with salt and freshly ground black pepper, often used to toss meat or fish prior to cooking.

Bouquet garni Used to flavour soups and casseroles. Can be bought, or make your own by tying together 1 sprig each of thyme and parsley, 1 bay leaf, a strip of lemon peel and 1 small celery stalk.

Herbs Use fresh unless specified otherwise. If you cannot obtain fresh for some of the recipes, substitute a smaller quantity of dried herbs.

Oven temperatures

The table below gives recommended equivalents.

	°C	°F	Gas Mark
Very cool	110	225	$\frac{1}{4}$
	120	250	$\frac{1}{2}$
Cool	140	275	1
	150	300	2
Moderate	160	325	3
	180	350	4
Moderately hot	190	375	5
	200	400	6
Hot	220	425	7
	230	450	8
Very hot	240	475	9

Notes for American and Australian users

In America the 8-oz measuring cup is used. In Australia metric measures are now used in conjunction with the standard 250-ml measuring cup. The Imperial pint, used in Britain and Australia, is 20 fl oz, while the American pint is 16 fl oz. It is important to remember that the Australian tablespoon differs from both the British and American tablespoons; the table below gives a comparison. The British standard tablespoon, which has been used throughout this book, holds 17.7 ml, the American 14.2 ml, and the Australian 20 ml. A teaspoon holds approximately 5 ml in all three countries.

British	American	Australian
1 teaspoon	1 teaspoon	1 teaspoon
1 tablespoon	1 tablespoon	1 tablespoon
2 tablespoons	3 tablespoons	2 tablespoons
$3\frac{1}{2}$ tablespoons	4 tablespoons	3 tablespoons
4 tablespoons	5 tablespoons	$3\frac{1}{2}$ tablespoons

Note: When making any of the recipes in this book, only follow one set of measures as they are not interchangeable.

American terms

The list below gives some American equivalents for terms used in this book.

British / American

baking tray / baking sheet
cake tin / cake pan
cling film / saran wrap
cocktail stick / toothpick
flan tin / pie pan
foil / aluminum foil
greaseproof paper / waxed paper
grill / broil

kitchen paper / paper towels
liquidise / blend
mince / grind
mould / mold
packet / package
piping bag / pastry bag
polythene / plastic
roasting tin / roasting pan

Introduction

No, *not* another boring book of diets, do's and don'ts. But an invitation to share the results of several years' cooking for an executive dining room for an employer on an enforced cholesterol lowering diet. At first it was very hard. It seemed to me an insult to expect anyone to cook well without butter, cream or eggs. My Irish upbringing made me imagine that such a régime would be emotionally as well as nutritionally depriving. Moreover I was steeped in the dogmas of French cuisine, and felt that to alter or depart from the essentials of a classical dish, by omitting butter or cream for instance, was heresy. I had never heard of 'la cuisine minceur' then – nor the word cholesterol, come to think of it!

But it was a challenge – and after a while the subject became totally absorbing. I started by studying the medical side at the library and then tackled the business of composing menus and recipes. I don't think our guests ever suspect that they are eating any sort of diet food. And far from being deprived, are glad to rise from the table, after a gourmet meal, without feeling like a Strasbourg goose, but with a clear mind and physically fit.

Cooking and eating are time-consuming operations, and low cholesterol cooking can be a chore – or a joy, depending on one's approach. The principles are really so simple as to be easily grasped by even an inexperienced cook, and the benefits are obvious; not solely to your heart, but also to figure and health. Once these principles have been understood the enthusiastic cook can develop the art of preserving the true and natural flavours of fresh food, and still keep an imaginative approach to cooking.

So many people now lead more sedentary lives than their grandparents used to; but without changing their diet accordingly. In particular, today's executive, who leads a stressful but physically inactive life, endangers his health with over-rich food and thinks he can buy more time on this earth with a few rounds of golf. Coronary disease is a major and increasing illness in this country, and the main contributory factors are high blood cholesterol level, high blood pressure and smoking. Doctors tell us also that we must begin young; good eating habits formed early will benefit your children for life. So safeguard the health, and particularly the hearts, of those you cook for.

Beth Cockman-Smith.

Cholesterol and the Diet

Heart disease is the most frequent cause of death in middle aged men, and the disease has reached epidemic proportions in the UK and other countries of the western world. It is not surprising, therefore, that men, and women, are concerned to do everything they can to prevent the disorder. The food we eat can play a part in altering blood fats, but there are many other factors which are important. For example, exercise is beneficial while smoking and overweight are risk factors.

In the context of diet, there is a lot of talk about animal fats, cholesterol and polyunsaturated fats. But these terms are often confused.

It is not necessary to know all the medical details to understand how to cook meals which will be good for *all* the family, including the children, but some facts will help.

Communities where there is a high incidence of heart disease frequently have a lot of cholesterol in their blood. And there is a large amount of cholesterol in the artery walls of people who have had a heart attack. For these two reasons medical authorities in many countries believe that we should try to reduce the amount of blood cholesterol. The food we eat can help to do this.

Food cholesterol

Animal foods like meat, milk, butter, hard cheese, cream and especially offal and eggs contain some ready-made cholesterol. This is a fatty substance which, in moderation, is essential for good health. But the amount of cholesterol we eat has only a small effect on the amount in the blood or body tissues because the body can manufacture cholesterol for itself. The amount made depends on several factors, but principally on the type of fat we eat.

Saturated fat

These are found mainly in animal foods – butter, cream, milk and hard cheeses, but also in coconut oil. Meats – especially lamb and beef – contain high amounts of saturated fats. Eating saturated fats enables the body to make more cholesterol than it needs, thus raising the blood level of cholesterol – something we are advised not to do! The amount of saturated fat we eat cannot be reduced to zero, but it can be cut down and partially replaced by polyunsaturated fats.

Polyunsaturated fats

These are found principally in vegetable foods and oils like corn oil, sunflower seed oil and safflower seed oil. Margarines made with a high proportion of these oils do not solidify in the refrigerator. Not only do they not raise blood cholesterol, they positively lower it. In other words, up to a point, the more polyunsaturated fat you eat, the lower your blood cholesterol gets.

But because it is very important to be slim, and fats are very high in energy, it is better to eat only moderate amounts of any fats.

Fish and fish oils are relatively rich in polyunsaturated fats, and chicken and other poultry are richer than beef and lamb. Pork comes between poultry and lamb.

The cholesterol lowering eating plan

There is every reason why the whole family should follow this eating plan – the sooner children learn good eating habits the better.

The overall aim is to reduce the amount of saturated fat and cholesterol eaten, replace some of this fat with polyunsaturated fat, and to be the correct weight for your height.

In terms of food this means:

Eat MORE chicken and fish (all types), eat MORE vegetables and fruit, MORE polyunsaturated margarine and corn or sunflower seed oil.
Eat NO butter, cream, whole milk and animal cooking fats.
Eat LESS offal, beef, lamb and egg yolk.

If you are overweight, start counting joules (or calories). Women on a slimming diet need about 5000 kilojoules (1200 calories) a day, men and children about 6300 kilojoules (1500 calories) a day. To guide you, the kilojoule/calorie count is given beside each recipe.

The following gives a more detailed breakdown of the foods to limit or avoid, the recommended foods to eat and the best ways to cook them.

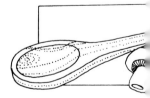

Meat and fish

Remove all visible fat from meat. Restrict meat to eight servings per week. Choose pork in preference to lamb. For the other main meals, concentrate on fish and poultry. Fish has a much lower fat content than meat and is a wonderful food for anyone on a cholesterol lowering diet. Bought minced beef can be fatty, so try to mince your own from leaner cuts of meat, and go easy on corned beef and tongue. Unfortunately, cholesterol is abundant in all offal; liver, heart, brains, kidneys, and sweetbreads; and also in shell-fish, such as prawns, and fish roes. But because liver and kidney are such good iron foods, either one may be eaten once a week.

Dairy produce and margarine

Avoid butter and cream. Substitute skimmed milk for whole milk. This can be bought from the milkman and some supermarkets, or you can make up your own from skimmed milk powder. Avoid non-dairy coffee creamers too. Limit most cheeses to 50 g/2 oz (US: ⅔ cup) per week. Edam and Gouda are low fat and 75 g/3 oz (US: 1 cup) may be eaten as an alternative to hard cheese. Skimmed milk cheeses such as cottage cheese or homemade curd cheese contain very little fat and need not be restricted. Low fat yogurt, natural and flavoured, is a boon in every way and can be used often.

Use the soft margarines that are clearly labelled 'high in polyunsaturates' for spreading on bread, tossing vegetables and for cooking. It may be sensible to limit the use of egg yolks to four per week, as these contain cholesterol. But opinion varies as to the importance of ready-made cholesterol in the diet; certainly the kind of fat you eat is much more important and relevant. So – within reason – don't be too strict about the number of eggs eaten. Of course, the whites are beyond suspicion and can be used freely. Make your own mayonnaise, eliminate ice creams and serve sorbets or slimmers' ice cream instead. Bake your own cakes and pastries using polyunsaturated fats.

Oils

Use the polyunsaturated oils. Sunflower, safflower and corn oils are recommended. Olive oil neither raises nor lowers blood cholesterol, so its *occasional* use in mayonnaise or salad dressing is permissible. Avoid unspecified vegetable oils and especially coconut or palm oil.

Fruit, vegetables and nuts

Fruit and vegetables are cholesterol free, so eat plenty of these with a clear conscience. Almost all nuts are good, particularly walnuts, hazelnuts and almonds, which are rich in polyunsaturates. But avoid coconut and cashew nuts.

Rice, pasta, pulses and cereals

These foods are an important source of vitamins, minerals and protein, and may be eaten regularly.

Cooking

Use the oils mentioned above for marinades and salad dressings; and these and the polyunsaturated margarines for frying, roasting, sauces, baking, etc. Yogurt is very valuable for thickening soups and sauces, in salad dressings, or as a delicious accompaniment to puddings and desserts. Curd cheese can be whizzed up in the liquidiser, or pressed through a sieve, to replace cream or cream cheese in some recipes.

Grill meats rather than fry, to encourage any fats to drip away from the food. Grilling and barbecuing can give fish and meat a delicious flavour, especially when the food has been previously marinated in a spicy sauce. If you must fry meats and fish, use as little extra fat as possible, and always drain the food afterwards on absorbent paper. By using a sauté pan with a lid, the food will cook more gently and absorb less fat.

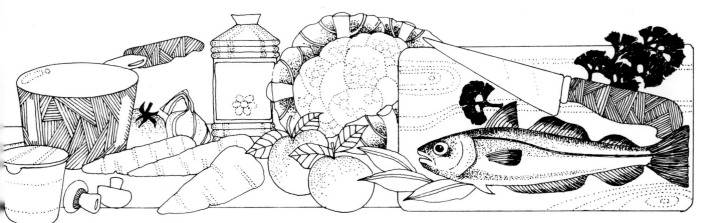

When roasting, stand the meat on a rack in a roasting tin, so the fats run into the tin and can be drained off. If you like, add a little stock or water to the tin to keep the meat moist during cooking, or cover with foil. Allow casseroles to cool then skim off any surface fat before reheating to serve. Always trim meat of excess fat before cooking.

Cooking in a brick is a wonderful way of keeping in the flavour and juices of meat or fish without adding fats. All good kitchen shops stock chicken or fish bricks, and there is now a larger brick which can take a joint of meat with vegetables. By first soaking the brick in cold water, the water evaporates into steam to keep the food moist and succulent during cooking.

I have been experimenting with good results with the 'cuisine minceur' methods of gently steaming fish, poultry or meat on a bed of finely chopped vegetables and herbs. It is important to have a really heavy, thick-bottomed casserole for this, with an extremely well-fitting lid to keep in all the moisture and aroma, and prevent the food from catching on the bottom. But this method uses the minimum of fat and retains all the essential nutrients and wonderful fresh flavour of the food.

Cooking 'en papillote' is also fun. Enclose food in a parcel of oiled greaseproof paper or foil and cook it in its own juices in the oven. It comes to the table in its wrapping and releases a marvellous smell when opened.

Cook food in season and allow yourself to be seduced by the lovely displays of fresh food in your greengrocer and fishmonger's. Try a delicious lunch of grilled fish, wholemeal bread and a green salad, or a slow, simmered casserole for supper. Casseroles are a great boon to the busy cook, as they separate the business of cooking and eating and have everyone sniffing the air in anticipation! Fresh vegetable soups are simple, delicious and nourishing. Wherever possible use fresh stock, it really does make all the difference to homemade dishes. Gently simmer a chicken carcass or some bones with whatever vegetables seem appropriate and are at hand; a carrot, stick of celery, an onion, a few parsley stalks, some mushroom stalks. Cool and skim before using.

When eating out

Try to follow the same pattern as for home cooking. Choose grilled meats and fish with vegetables or a salad, and a sorbet or fruit to follow. Avoid rich sauces and dressings, and hidden fats in pastries, cakes and gâteaux. Drink your coffee *without* cream!

The Rating System

All the recipes in this book have been rated to guide you in your menu planning.

♥   These dishes may be eaten as often as you like – providing you are not trying to lose weight! They are rich in poly-unsaturated fats and contain very little cholesterol.

♥ ♥   You may eat up to 5 of these dishes a week. They are not quite as rich in poly-unsaturates as ♥ recipes.

♥ ♥ ♥   Eat up to 3 of these a week. Although they have more saturated fat than poly-unsaturated, there is no reason why you should not eat a certain amount. Besides, the foods contained in some of these recipes contain other valuable nutrients which promote good health.

This guide to choosing foods is intended for people who are not receiving advice from a doctor. It may well be that if a doctor has prescribed a diet for you there will be other rules. Do observe them.

If you need to lose weight, keep an eye on the joule (or calorie) figures as well as the rating. Food energy has traditionally been measured in calories, but the International System of Units uses the kilojoule. In this book, the Imperial recipes are calorie counted and the metric recipes are kilojoule counted. (As a rough guide 1000 calories is equivalent to 4200 kilojoules).

The recipes in this book aim to cater for every taste and every occasion, from the simplest to the most exotic. So enjoy trying out the new ideas and recipes and above all enjoy eating the delicious results!

Which Foods?

What kinds of foods should you eat and which should you try to avoid? There is no absolutely certain list of the good and the bad foods because people have their own ideas, but the following table will act as a guide. It assumes that you do not have to lose weight. If you do, clearly you will have to restrict some of the fatty and high sugar foods in the first column.

	As often as you like	In moderation		Very strictly controlled
Fruit and vegetables	all fruit and vegetables, fresh, frozen, dried or canned	avocado pears olives		
Dairy produce, fats and oils	polyunsaturated margarine corn, sunflower seed and safflower seed oils cottage cheese low fat yogurt skimmed milk egg whites	olive oil hard cheese (50 g/2 oz/ ⅔ cup per week) coffee creamers whole eggs – up to four per week		lard butter non-polyunsaturated margarines dripping unspecified vegetable oils and white fats cream cheese cream whole milk
Nuts	most nuts	coconut, cashews		
Meat	chicken turkey vegetable protein	beef bacon pork lamb ham sausages cold cuts canned meats	*up to eight servings per week*	tongue black sausage offal
Fish	white fish oily fish canned fish			shellfish cods' roe
Cereals, sweets and sundries	sugar jams, jellies, honey slimmers' ice cream (made without any fat) flour, bread breakfast cereals pasta, rice coffee, tea salt, spices	alcohol		chocolate toffees dairy ice cream manufactured baked goods like cakes, biscuits (unless you know they are made with polyunsaturated fats)

Starters

Set the standard for the meal to follow with any of these unusual and appetising openers. Tiny button mushrooms cooked in cider, savoury stuffed peppers or tomatoes, an assortment of quiches and a genuine Norwegian recipe for home-cured salmon, are just some of the starters that would make equally delicious light luncheon or supper dishes.

Tomates Farcies Duxelles (see recipe page 12)
Mushrooms en Cocotte (see recipe page 12)

Mushrooms en Cocotte

(illustrated on pages 10–11)

Per portion: 650 kilojoules/160 calories
Serves 4 ♥

METRIC/IMPERIAL	AMERICAN
0.5 kg/1 lb button mushrooms	1 lb button mushrooms
1 tablespoon polyunsaturated oil	1 tablespoon polyunsaturated oil
25 g/1 oz polyunsaturated margarine	2 tablespoons polyunsaturated margarine
1 heaped tablespoon flour	1 heaped tablespoon all-purpose flour
300 ml/½ pint cider	1¼ cups cider
salt and freshly ground black pepper	salt and freshly ground black pepper
2 tablespoons fresh breadcrumbs	3 tablespoons fresh soft bread crumbs
parsley sprigs to garnish	parsley sprigs to garnish

Grease four individual ovenproof dishes.

Sauté the mushrooms for a few minutes in the oil and margarine. Sprinkle on the flour and mix in gently. Add the cider slowly, mixing all together, and bring to the boil, stirring. Season to taste. Spoon into the ramekins and sprinkle over the breadcrumbs. Dot with a little more margarine and toast to a golden brown under the grill. Serve garnished with parsley.

Tomates Farcies Duxelles

(illustrated on pages 10–11)

Per portion: 920 kilojoules/230 calories
Serves 6 ♥

METRIC/IMPERIAL	AMERICAN
6 medium mushrooms	6 medium mushrooms
1 shallot or small onion	1 shallot or small onion
1 stick celery	1 stalk celery
1 tablespoon polyunsaturated oil	1 tablespoon polyunsaturated oil
50 g/2 oz polyunsaturated margarine	¼ cup polyunsaturated margarine
1 teaspoon chopped basil (or ½ teaspoon dried basil)	1 teaspoon chopped basil (or ½ teaspoon dried basil)
1 tablespoon chopped parsley	1 tablespoon chopped parsley
½ teaspoon chopped lemon thyme	½ teaspoon chopped lemon thyme
4 tablespoons fresh white breadcrumbs	⅓ cup fresh soft white bread crumbs
salt and freshly ground black pepper	salt and freshly ground black pepper
6 firm tomatoes	6 firm tomatoes
6 rounds toast	6 rounds toast
polyunsaturated margarine to spread	polyunsaturated margarine to spread
1 small clove garlic, crushed	1 small clove garlic, crushed
parsley sprigs to garnish	parsley sprigs to garnish

Clean and peel the mushrooms and remove stalks. Chop peelings and stalks finely and keep on one side. Finely chop the shallot and celery. Heat half the oil and margarine and cook the shallot and celery, very slowly. Add the duxelles (mushroom peelings and stalks) and continue to cook over a low heat until everything is soft (about 7 minutes). Add the herbs and breadcrumbs and continue cooking, turning everything about in the pan, until the breadcrumbs have begun to brown. Season to taste.

Cut the tops off the tomatoes and scoop out the seeds and juice; drain the tomatoes upside down for a minute. Fry the mushroom caps in the remaining oil and margarine. Stuff the tomatoes with the breadcrumb mixture and top each with a fried mushroom cap. Place the tomatoes on rounds of toasted bread, spread with garlic 'butter'. Cover with greased foil and bake in a hot oven (220°C, 425°F, Gas Mark 7) for 10 minutes. Garnish with parsley.

Smoked Fish

♥

Good Scotch smoked salmon is always delicious, and a great compliment to your guests; but it is very expensive now, so it is worth experimenting with some of the other varieties of smoked fish. Smoked trout is served with horseradish, and smoked mackerel and buckling are cheaper and both good. Smoked eels are some people's passion – but they are very much a matter of personal taste.

Served with a selection of the following: brown bread and polyunsaturated margarine, lemon wedges, horseradish sauce and lettuce hearts.

Fresh Tomato Juice Cocktail

A really refreshing starter. Make this when tomatoes are plentiful.

Per portion: 150 kilojoules/35 calories
Serves 8 ♥

METRIC/IMPERIAL
1.75 kg/4 lb ripe tomatoes
1 teaspoon sugar
juice of 1 small lemon
good twist of lemon peel
2 teaspoons Worcestershire sauce
3 drops Tabasco sauce
1 teaspoon salt
freshly ground black pepper
Garnish
lemon slices
watercress sprigs

AMERICAN
4 lb ripe tomatoes
1 teaspoon sugar
juice of 1 small lemon
good twist of lemon peel
2 teaspoons Worcestershire sauce
3 drops Tabasco sauce
1 teaspoon salt
freshly ground black pepper
Garnish
lemon slices
watercress sprigs

Roughly chop the tomatoes. Place in the liquidiser with the sugar. Blend and sieve. Pour the juice into a glass jug with the remaining ingredients and chill for several hours, for the lemon peel to infuse its flavour.

Pour into individual glasses and garnish each with a lemon slice and small sprig of watercress.

Melon with Vermouth

Per portion: 450 kilojoules/110 calories
Serves 4 ♥

METRIC/IMPERIAL
1 small melon
4 oranges, segmented
4 tablespoons white vermouth
1 egg white
castor sugar
4 sprigs mint

AMERICAN
1 small melon
4 oranges, segmented
⅓ cup white vermouth
1 egg white
sugar
4 sprigs mint

Scoop out the flesh from the melon with a small ball cutter. Place in a bowl with the orange segments (free from pith or membrane) and pour over the vermouth. Cover and chill.

Dip the rims of four glasses first into the lightly whisked egg white, then into castor sugar, to make a pretty frosted rim. To serve, turn the melon mixture into the prepared glasses and garnish each with a mint sprig.

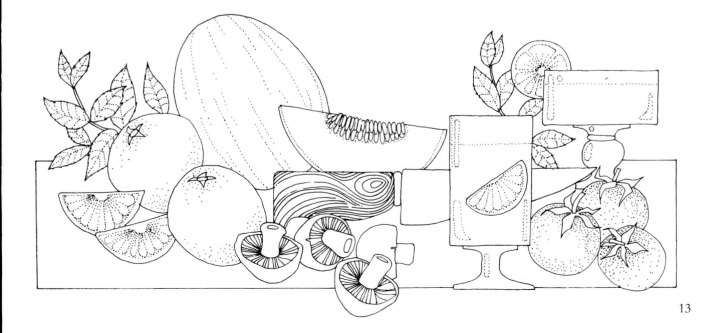

Tagliatelle Romana

(illustrated opposite)

My version of a marvellous pasta dish served in a little Roman restaurant.

Per portion : 1420 kilojoules/345 calories
Serves 4 ♥

METRIC/IMPERIAL	AMERICAN
225 g/8 oz tagliatelle noodles	½ lb tagliatelle noodles
chicken stock	chicken stock
2 tablespoons polyunsaturated oil	3 tablespoons polyunsaturated oil
50 g/2 oz smoked prosciutto ham	¼ cup chopped prosciutto ham
100 g/4 oz curd cheese (see page 64)	½ cup curd cheese (see page 64)
1 clove garlic, crushed	1 clove garlic, crushed
salt and freshly ground black pepper	salt and freshly ground black pepper

Cook the tagliatelle in plenty of chicken stock until just tender. Drain, turn into a hot dish and toss with the oil.

Remove any fat from the prosciutto and cut the meat into strips. Sieve the curd cheese and mix in the garlic and seasoning. Stir the cheese mixture into the tagliatelle, finally toss in the ham strips and serve immediately.

Pizza Quiche

(illustrated on page 63)

This is very good, and contains no eggs. The black olives and red of the tomatoes look very effective together.

Per portion : 1555 kilojoules/370 calories
Serves 6 ♥

METRIC/IMPERIAL	AMERICAN
175 g/6 oz quantity easy mix pastry with oil (see page 62)	6 oz quantity easy mix pastry with oil (see page 62)
1 (56-g/2-oz) can anchovy fillets	1 (2-oz) can anchovy fillets
2 large Spanish onions, chopped	2 large Spanish onions, chopped
3 tablespoons pure corn oil	¼ cup pure corn oil
6 large ripe tomatoes, peeled and chopped	6 large ripe tomatoes, peeled and chopped
salt and freshly ground black pepper	salt and freshly ground black pepper
pinch sugar	pinch sugar
1 tablespoon tomato purée	1 tablespoon tomato paste
1 teaspoon dried oregano	1 teaspoon dried oregano
black olives	ripe olives
pure corn oil to sprinkle	pure corn oil to sprinkle

Line a 20-cm/8-inch (US: 8-inch) flan tin with the pastry and bake blind in a moderately hot oven (200°C, 400°F, Gas Mark 6) for 15 minutes.

Halve the anchovy fillets lengthways and soak in milk.

Cook the onions in the oil until soft but not brown, then add the chopped tomatoes, seasoning, sugar, tomato purée and oregano. Cook gently for about 5 minutes, mashing the tomatoes slightly with a wooden spoon. Turn into the prepared pastry case, spreading over. Drain the anchovies and arrange in a lattice over the tomato mixture. Put one black olive in each of the squares and sprinkle over a little oil. Bake in a moderate oven (180°C, 350°F, Gas Mark 4) for about 20 minutes.

Avocado and Caviar Mousse

Per portion : 325 kilojoules/80 calories
Serves 4 ♥ ♥

METRIC/IMPERIAL	AMERICAN
1 avocado pear	1 avocado
juice of ½ lemon	juice of ½ lemon
few drops garlic juice	few drops garlic juice
75 g/3 oz curd cheese (see page 64)	6 tablespoons curd cheese (see page 64)
salt and freshly ground black pepper	salt and freshly ground black pepper
1 (58-g/2-oz) jar Danish caviar	1 (2-oz) jar Danish caviar

Halve the avocado and remove the flesh with a teaspoon. Put into a bowl with the lemon juice, and beat in the garlic juice and sieved cheese until smooth. Season to taste and gently fold in the caviar.

Serve on a plain white dish, surrounded by crisp lettuce leaves, with fingers of hot toast.

Tagliatelle Romana (see recipe above)

Gravad Lax

This is my Norwegian mother-in-law's recipe for home-cured salmon, which in Norway is considered more of a delicacy than smoked salmon. If you are economising, buy the tailpiece of the salmon, and negotiate a good price with your fishmonger. A fresh mackerel is also excellent treated in the same way, head removed and filleted.

Per portion: 900 kilojoules/230 calories
Serves 8 ♥

METRIC/IMPERIAL	AMERICAN
1 kg/2 lb piece of salmon, or 1 large mackerel	2 lb piece of salmon, or 1 large mackerel
juice of 1 small lemon	juice of 1 small lemon
For the mixture	*For the mixture*
1 heaped tablespoon salt	1½ tablespoons salt
1 heaped tablespoon castor sugar	1½ tablespoons sugar
1 tablespoon crushed black peppercorns	1 tablespoon crushed black peppercorns
2 heaped tablespoons chopped dill	3 tablespoons chopped dill

Mix together the ingredients for the mixture. Lay a large piece of cling film or foil on a plate and spread on a quarter of this mixture, to an area the size of the fish. Over it lay the opened-out fish, skin side down. Remove any remaining fish bones then spread over half the mixture. Fold to make a fish shape again, and spread the remaining quarter of the mixture on top. Close up the cling film or foil and seal to make a neat parcel. Cover with a weight on a board.

Leave in the refrigerator for 3–4 days, turning the parcel twice a day. Unwrap and drain. Sprinkle with the lemon juice. Serve, in thin slices, with lemon wedges and chopped dill, and plenty of brown bread and polyunsaturated margarine. *Note:* This dish freezes well. Drain thoroughly and wrap in fresh cling film.

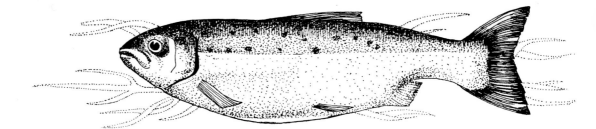

Spinach Quiche

Per portion: 1410 kilojoules/375 calories
Serves 8 ♥

METRIC/IMPERIAL	AMERICAN
For the pastry	*For the pastry*
100 g/4 oz flour	1 cup all-purpose flour
100 g/4 oz polyunsaturated margarine	½ cup polyunsaturated margarine
100 g/4 oz roast hazelnuts, ground	¾ cup roast hazelnuts, ground
½ teaspoon salt	½ teaspoon salt
½ teaspoon dried mixed herbs	½ teaspoon dried mixed herbs
2 tablespoons skimmed milk	3 tablespoons skimmed milk
For the filling	*For the filling*
4–5 spring onions	4–5 scallions
50 g/2 oz polyunsaturated margarine	¼ cup polyunsaturated margarine
1 tablespoon flour	1 tablespoon all-purpose flour
225 g/8 oz chopped cooked spinach	1 cup chopped cooked spinach
salt and freshly ground black pepper	salt and freshly ground black pepper
225 g/8 oz cottage cheese	1 cup cottage cheese
pinch grated nutmeg	pinch grated nutmeg
2 tablespoons grated Parmesan cheese	3 tablespoons grated Parmesan cheese
2 egg whites	2 egg whites

Make the pastry following the method for basic shortcrust (see page 62), adding the ground hazelnuts, salt and herbs with the remaining flour, and substituting skimmed milk for the water. Line a 25-cm/10-inch (US: 10-inch) flan tin with the pastry, cover with greaseproof paper and fill with baking beans. Bake blind for 15 minutes in a moderately hot oven (200°C, 400°F, Gas Mark 6).

Meanwhile finely chop the spring onions, discarding the green parts. Fry gently in the margarine until softened. Stir in the flour. Drain the spinach thoroughly and add to the onions. Cook for a few minutes, stirring. Season well and add the cottage cheese, nutmeg and Parmesan cheese. Fold in the stiffly whisked egg whites and pile into the pastry shell. Return to the oven and bake at 190°C, 375°F, Gas Mark 5 for 30 minutes.

Hazelnut and Leek Quiche

*Per portion: 1625 kilojoules/440 calories
Serves 8* ♥

METRIC/IMPERIAL
For the pastry
100 g/4 oz flour
100 g/4 oz polyunsaturated margarine
100 g/4 oz roast hazelnuts, ground
½ teaspoon salt
½ teaspoon dried marjoram
2 tablespoons skimmed milk
For the filling
4 large leeks
50 g/2 oz polyunsaturated margarine
2 tablespoons flour
300 ml/½ pint skimmed milk
3 tablespoons grated low fat cheese
(Edam or Gouda)
2 tablespoons grated Parmesan cheese
salt and freshly ground black pepper
4 tablespoons fresh breadcrumbs
½ teaspoon dried marjoram
polyunsaturated oil to sprinkle

AMERICAN
For the pastry
1 cup all-purpose flour
½ cup polyunsaturated margarine
¾ cup roast hazelnuts, ground
½ teaspoon salt
½ teaspoon dried marjoram
3 tablespoons skimmed milk
For the filling
4 large leeks
¼ cup polyunsaturated margarine
3 tablespoons all-purpose flour
1¼ cups skimmed milk
¼ cup grated low fat cheese
(Edam or Gouda)
3 tablespoons grated Parmesan cheese
salt and freshly ground black pepper
⅓ cup fresh soft bread crumbs
½ teaspoon dried marjoram
polyunsaturated oil to sprinkle

Make the pastry, use to line a 25-cm/10-inch (US: 10-inch) flan tin and bake blind, all as for Spinach Quiche (see page 16).

Chop the white part of the leeks, wash and clean thoroughly. Cook for about 10 minutes in boiling salted water. Drain well.

Melt the margarine, stir in the flour and cook for 1 minute. Gradually add the milk and bring to the boil, stirring all the time. Stir in the cheeses and season to taste. Fold the leeks into the cheese sauce and pour into the prepared pastry case. Mix the breadcrumbs with the marjoram and use to top the quiche. Sprinkle over a little oil. Bake in a moderately hot oven (190°C, 375°F, Gas Mark 5) for 30 minutes.

Stuffed Green Peppers

*Per portion: 985 kilojoules/235 calories
Serves 6* ♥

METRIC/IMPERIAL
6 green peppers
175 g/6 oz long-grain rice
rind and juice of 1 large lemon
3 tablespoons chopped herbs (parsley,
chives and thyme)
150 ml/¼ pint French dressing, made with
6 tablespoons polyunsaturated oil, the
lemon juice, ½ teaspoon each sugar, salt
and pepper (see page 60)

AMERICAN
6 green peppers
¾ cup long-grain rice
rind and juice of 1 large lemon
¼ cup chopped herbs (parsley, chives
and thyme)
⅔ cup French dressing, made with ½ cup
polyunsaturated oil, the lemon juice,
½ teaspoon each sugar, salt and pepper
(see page 60)

Slice the lids off the peppers and carefully remove all seeds and pith from inside. Wash and blanch for 6 minutes in boiling water, then plunge immediately into cold water, to keep the fresh colour. Drain and pat dry with kitchen paper.

Boil the rice in plenty of salted water for 10 minutes. Drain and cool. Flavour the rice with the grated lemon rind and chopped herbs. Toss with French dressing and pile into the peppers. Replace the pepper lids. Finally pour a little French dressing over the peppers and serve.

Soups

Warming winter soups, simple summer soups, various vegetable soups and even exotic soups. As a way of bringing out the true flavour of fresh vegetables, or turning an assortment of ingredients into a tempting, wholesome dish, soups are unbeatable.

French Onion Soup (see recipe page 20)
Winter Vegetable Soup (see recipe page 20)
Walnut Soup (see recipe page 20)

Walnut Soup

(illustrated on pages 18–19)

Per portion: 730 kilojoules/170 calories
Serves 6 ♥

METRIC/IMPERIAL
175 g/6 oz shelled walnuts
1 clove garlic, crushed
900 ml/1½ pints hot chicken stock,
made up with 2 stock cubes
salt and white pepper
150 ml/¼ pint natural low fat yogurt
watercress sprigs to garnish

AMERICAN
1½ cups shelled walnuts
1 clove garlic, crushed
3¾ cups hot chicken stock,
made up with 2 stock cubes
salt and white pepper
⅔ cup plain low fat yogurt
watercress sprigs to garnish

Put the walnuts and garlic into the liquidiser with a little stock, and blend to a creamy consistency. Turn into a saucepan, gradually stir in the remaining stock and heat through. Season to taste.

Remove from the heat and stir in the yogurt. Serve garnished with small sprigs of watercress.

French Onion Soup

(illustrated on pages 18–19)

Per portion: 1560 kilojoules/385 calories
Serves 6 ♥

METRIC/IMPERIAL
3 large Spanish onions, finely chopped
3 tablespoons polyunsaturated oil
generous litre/2 pints beef stock,
made up with 2 stock cubes
1 teaspoon sugar
salt and freshly ground black pepper
6 slices French bread
polyunsaturated margarine to spread
100 g/4 oz Edam cheese, grated
1 tablespoon brandy
chopped parsley to garnish

AMERICAN
3 large Spanish onions, finely chopped
¼ cup polyunsaturated oil
2½ pints beef stock,
made up with 2 stock cubes
1 teaspoon sugar
salt and freshly ground black pepper
6 slices French bread
polyunsaturated margarine to spread
1 cup grated Edam cheese
1 tablespoon brandy
chopped parsley to garnish

Cook the onions in the oil in a thick-bottomed, covered pan for at least 30 minutes, turning frequently. They should not brown, but should be quite soft. Boil with the stock, sugar, salt and pepper for a further 30 minutes.

Meanwhile, toast the bread slices in the oven, spread with margarine, heap the grated cheese on top and brown under the grill. Now stir the brandy into the soup, and serve with a cheesy bread slice in each bowl. Sprinkle with chopped parsley.

Winter Vegetable Soup

(illustrated on pages 18–19)

Per portion: 575 kilojoules/150 calories
Serves 6 ♥

METRIC/IMPERIAL
50 g/2 oz polyunsaturated margarine
225 g/8 oz carrots, chopped
225 g/8 oz parsnips, chopped
175 g/6 oz turnips, chopped
175 g/6 oz swede, chopped
generous litre/2 pints chicken or beef
stock, made up with 2 stock cubes
2 tablespoons chopped parsley
salt and freshly ground black pepper
grated Edam cheese to serve

AMERICAN
4 tablespoons polyunsaturated margarine
½ lb carrots, chopped
½ lb parsnips, chopped
1 cup chopped turnip
1 cup chopped swede
5 cups chicken or beef stock,
made up with 2 stock cubes
3 tablespoons chopped parsley
salt and freshly ground black pepper
grated Edam cheese to serve

Melt the margarine in a heavy-bottomed saucepan and add all the chopped vegetables. Cook gently, stirring, for 10 minutes. Add the stock to the vegetables and bring to the boil. Cover and simmer for 15–20 minutes, until the vegetables are tender. Add the parsley and season to taste.

Hand the grated cheese separately, a little to be sprinkled on the top of each serving.

Artichoke Soup

Per portion: 700 kilojoules/180 calories
Serves 6 ♥

METRIC/IMPERIAL	AMERICAN
0.5 kg/1 lb Jerusalem artichokes	1 lb Jerusalem artichokes
1 tablespoon polyunsaturated oil	1 tablespoon polyunsaturated oil
50 g/2 oz polyunsaturated margarine	¼ cup polyunsaturated margarine
generous litre/2 pints skimmed milk	2½ pints skimmed milk
salt and white pepper	salt and white pepper
chopped parsley to garnish	chopped parsley to garnish
croûtons to serve	croûtons to serve

Carefully scrape and chop the artichokes. Cook gently in the oil and margarine in a heavy-bottomed saucepan, stirring frequently, until soft. Add a little milk if they start to turn brown. When soft, blend the artichokes in the liquidiser with some of the milk, or press through a sieve. Return the purée to the saucepan, stir in the remaining milk and bring to the boil. Cover and simmer for 10 minutes. Taste and adjust for seasoning and sprinkle over chopped parsley.

Serve with plenty of croûtons (small crustless cubes of bread fried in poly-unsaturated oil and margarine until golden, then drained on absorbent paper).

Fresh Tomato Soup

The simplest and best method I know.

Per portion: 495 kilojoules/125 calories
Serves 8 ♥

METRIC/IMPERIAL	AMERICAN
1 kg/2 lb ripe tomatoes, roughly chopped	2 lb ripe tomatoes, roughly chopped
1 small onion, chopped	1 small onion, chopped
2 tablespoons polyunsaturated oil	3 tablespoons polyunsaturated oil
50 g/2 oz polyunsaturated margarine	¼ cup polyunsaturated margarine
1 sugar cube	1 sugar cube
1 orange	1 orange
1.75 litres/3 pints light stock (chicken, turkey or veal)	4 pints light stock (chicken, turkey or veal)
2 cloves	2 cloves
bouquet garni	bouquet garni

Soften the tomatoes and onion in the oil and margarine for about 8 minutes. Rub the sugar cube over the orange zest, to absorb the flavour, and add with the remaining ingredients to the tomato mixture. Bring to the boil, cover and simmer gently for 25 minutes. Remove the cloves and bouquet garni.

Blend the soup in a liquidiser then push with a wooden spoon through a fine sieve. Reheat and serve.

The subtle orange flavour really does make all the difference to this delicious soup.

Spinach Soup

Per portion: 625 kilojoules/150 calories
Serves 4 ♥

METRIC/IMPERIAL	AMERICAN
1 small onion, chopped	1 small onion, chopped
2 tablespoons polyunsaturated oil	3 tablespoons polyunsaturated oil
1 tablespoon flour	1 tablespoon all-purpose flour
225 g/8 oz finely chopped frozen spinach, defrosted	½ lb finely chopped frozen spinach, thawed
600 ml/1 pint chicken or veal stock	2½ cups chicken or veal stock
150 ml/¼ pint natural low fat yogurt	⅔ cup plain low fat yogurt

Soften the onion in the oil. Stir in the flour and cook for 1 minute. Stir in the spinach and cook over low heat for 3 minutes, stirring. Add the stock, bring to the boil, cover and simmer gently for 10 minutes.

Just before serving, remove from the heat and stir in the yogurt.

Courgette and Cucumber Soup

Per portion: 105 kilojoules/25 calories
Serves 4 ♥

METRIC/IMPERIAL
1 cucumber, roughly chopped
equal weight in courgettes, chopped
900 ml/1½ pints chicken stock
snipped chives to garnish

AMERICAN
1 cucumber, roughly chopped
equal weight in courgettes, chopped
3¾ cups chicken stock
snipped chives to garnish

Simmer the cucumber and courgettes in the stock for 15 minutes. Blend in the liquidiser or press through a sieve. Reheat or serve chilled with a pinch of chives.

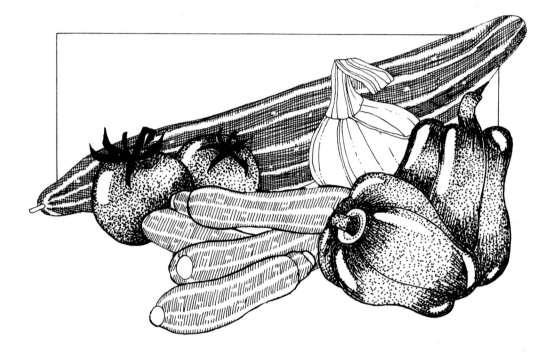

Gazpacho

(illustrated opposite)

A Spanish favourite.

Per portion: 710 kilojoules/170 calories
Serves 8 ♥

METRIC/IMPERIAL
4 large ripe tomatoes, peeled and deseeded
½ Spanish onion, sliced
2 small green peppers, chopped
1 cucumber, diced
450 ml/¾ pint tomato juice
1 clove garlic, chopped
6 tablespoons pure corn oil
4 tablespoons lemon juice
salt and freshly ground black pepper
1 teaspoon sugar
8 ice cubes
Garnish
2 slices bread, diced
2 tomatoes, peeled and quartered
diced green pepper
diced cucumber
½ Spanish onion

AMERICAN
4 large ripe tomatoes, peeled and deseeded
½ Spanish onion, sliced
2 small green peppers, chopped
1 cucumber diced
2 cups tomato juice
1 clove garlic, chopped
½ cup pure corn oil
⅓ cup lemon juice
salt and freshly ground black pepper
1 teaspoon sugar
8 ice cubes
Garnish
2 slices bread, diced
2 tomatoes, peeled and quartered
diced green pepper
diced cucumber
½ Spanish onion

Blend in the liquidiser the tomatoes, onion, peppers (keeping some aside for the garnish), cucumber (keeping some for garnish), tomato juice, garlic, oil, lemon juice, seasoning and sugar. Chill. Just before serving, add the ice cubes.

Accompany the large bowl of gazpacho with small bowls of toasted diced bread, tomatoes and pepper, cucumber and onion rings.

22

Gazpacho (see recipe above)

Iced Cucumber Soup

Per portion: 650 kilojoules/160 calories
Serves 6 ♥

METRIC/IMPERIAL
1 small onion, finely chopped
2 tablespoons polyunsaturated oil
25 g/1 oz polyunsaturated margarine
1 large cucumber, peeled and sliced
4 medium potatoes, sliced
900 ml/1½ pints light chicken stock
salt and white pepper
2 tablespoons natural low fat yogurt
chopped mint to garnish

AMERICAN
1 small onion, finely chopped
3 tablespoons polyunsaturated oil
2 tablespoons polyunsaturated margarine
1 large cucumber, peeled and sliced
4 medium potatoes, sliced
3¾ cups light chicken stock
salt and white pepper
3 tablespoons plain low fat yogurt
chopped mint to garnish

Soften the onion in the oil and margarine, then add the cucumber and potato. Cook very gently for 10 minutes, stirring from time to time, without browning. Add the stock and bring to the boil. Cover and simmer gently for 20 minutes (not more).

Press through a sieve or blend in the liquidiser and pour into a bowl to cool. Adjust seasoning when the soup is cold. Just before serving, stir in the yogurt and garnish with chopped mint. Serve chilled with hot crusty rolls.

Vichyssoise

This is an elegant chilled soup, an ideal starter for a summer dinner party. Served hot, with skimmed milk in place of the yogurt, it becomes Potage Bonne Femme, a comforting and delicious winter soup.

Per portion: 830 kilojoules/200 calories
Serves 6 ♥

METRIC/IMPERIAL
4 large leeks
1 small onion, chopped
2 tablespoons polyunsaturated oil
4 medium potatoes, sliced
600 ml/1 pint chicken stock
salt and white pepper
150 ml/¼ pint natural low fat yogurt
snipped chives to garnish

AMERICAN
4 large leeks
1 small onion, chopped
3 tablespoons polyunsaturated oil
4 medium potatoes, sliced
2½ cups chicken stock
salt and white pepper
⅔ cup plain low fat yogurt
snipped chives to garnish

Wash, trim and chop the leeks. Soften with the onion in the oil, without browning. Add the potatoes and cook gently for a further 5 minutes. Pour in the stock and season to taste. Bring to the boil, cover and simmer for 20 minutes. Press through a sieve or blend in the liquidiser. Cool and stir in the yogurt.

Serve chilled, sprinkled with chives.

Country Vegetable Soup

Per portion: 465 kilojoules/115 calories
Serves 6 ♥

METRIC/IMPERIAL
1 small onion, chopped
2 leeks, washed, trimmed and sliced
3 sticks celery, sliced
1 tablespoon polyunsaturated oil
25 g/1 oz polyunsaturated margarine
350 g/12 oz ripe tomatoes, peeled and chopped
generous litre/2 pints light chicken or vegetable stock
225 g/8 oz potatoes, sliced
1 clove garlic, chopped
salt and pepper
pinch cayenne pepper

AMERICAN
1 small onion, chopped
2 leeks, washed, trimmed and sliced
3 stalks celery, sliced
1 tablespoon polyunsaturated oil
2 tablespoons polyunsaturated margarine
¾ lb ripe tomatoes, peeled and chopped
2½ pints light chicken or vegetable stock
½ lb potatoes, sliced
1 clove garlic, chopped
salt and pepper
pinch cayenne pepper

Soften the onion, leeks and celery in the oil and margarine, but do not brown. Add the tomatoes and stock, then the potatoes and garlic. Bring to the boil, stirring occasionally. Cover and simmer for about 30 minutes, until the vegetables are tender. Sieve or blend in the liquidiser until smooth. If the soup seems too thick, add a little more stock.

Return to the pan, reheat and adjust for seasoning. Add a pinch of cayenne to serve.

Carrot and Tomato Soup

Per portion: 610 kilojoules/150 calories
Serves 8 ♥

METRIC/IMPERIAL
1 tablespoon polyunsaturated oil
75 g/3 oz polyunsaturated margarine
1 medium onion, chopped
1 kg/2 lb ripe tomatoes, chopped
225 g/8 oz carrots, grated
2 sugar cubes
2 oranges
scant 1.5 litres/2½ pints stock (light chicken or vegetable)
6 peppercorns
1 small bay leaf
1 clove
salt and pepper

AMERICAN
1 tablespoon polyunsaturated oil
6 tablespoons polyunsaturated margarine
1 medium onion, chopped
2 lb ripe tomatoes, chopped
½ lb carrots, grated
2 sugar cubes
2 oranges
6¼ cups stock (light chicken or vegetable)
6 peppercorns
1 small bay leaf
1 clove
salt and pepper

Heat the oil and margarine in a large, heavy-bottomed pan. Add the onion, cover and cook gently for a few minutes. Add the tomatoes and carrots and cook slowly, still covered, for about 10 minutes, stirring occasionally. Rub the sugar cubes over the oranges to absorb the flavour, then add with the stock. Bring to the boil, cover and simmer for 20 minutes.

Give it a quick jizz in the liquidiser, then sieve the soup into a clean pan. Stir in the juice squeezed from the oranges, the peppercorns, bay leaf and clove. Leave these last three ingredients to infuse for about 1 hour if possible, then remove. Taste and adjust for seasoning. Heat through and strain into a hot tureen to serve.

Cooking in a brick is one way of cooking fish to perfection. But not the only way. Try mackerel with yogurt and chives, a Norwegian dish, deceptively simple and quite delicious; or psari plaki, fish baked in the oven with oil and herbs, the Greek way. Kedgeree, fish pie and trout with almonds are already favourites and need no recommendation – and don't forget that fish is a wonderfully nourishing food for anyone on a low cholesterol diet.

Fish in a Brick (see recipe page 28)

Fish in a Brick

(illustrated on pages 26–27)

One of the Venetian ways of preparing fish is to bake them in earthenware in the oven, with oil and herbs and lemon, and then to serve them cold, with more oil, herbs and lemon. Mackerel, red mullet or grey mullet are suitable fish.

Per portion: 1585 kilojoules/380 calories
Serves 2 ♥

METRIC/IMPERIAL	AMERICAN
1 large fish, cleaned	1 large fish, cleaned
2 tablespoons pure corn oil	3 tablespoons pure corn oil
1 bay leaf, crumbled	1 bay leaf, crumbled
2 teaspoons finely chopped parsley	2 teaspoons finely chopped parsley
2 teaspoons finely chopped thyme or fennel	2 teaspoons finely chopped thyme or fennel
1 lemon, sliced	1 lemon, sliced
1 clove garlic, crushed	1 clove garlic, crushed
salt and freshly ground black pepper	salt and freshly ground black pepper

First soak a fish brick in cold water for 10 minutes. Remove.

Make a few incisions in the uppermost side of the fish. Mix together the oil, herbs, lemon slices, garlic and seasoning. Sprinkle half this mixture inside the fish and over the cuts. Rub the underside with a little extra oil. Lay the fish in the brick and replace the cover. Put the brick into a cold oven and set to 190°C, 375°F, Gas Mark 5. Cook for about 1 hour. Allow to cool and serve with the remaining oil and herb mixture poured over.

A potato salad and a tomato salad would accompany this well.

Note: If you do not have a fish brick, this dish can be successfully made wrapped in foil in a roasting tin.

Portuguese Cod

Per portion: 990 kilojoules/240 calories
Serves 4 ♥

METRIC/IMPERIAL	AMERICAN
1 onion, chopped	1 onion, chopped
1 tablespoon polyunsaturated oil	1 tablespoon polyunsaturated oil
25 g/1 oz polyunsaturated margarine	2 tablespoons polyunsaturated margarine
1 clove garlic, crushed	1 clove garlic, crushed
4 tomatoes, peeled and chopped	4 tomatoes, peeled and chopped
juice of 1 lemon	juice of 1 lemon
salt and freshly ground black pepper	salt and freshly ground black pepper
4 individual cod steaks	4 individual cod steaks
chopped parsley to garnish	chopped parsley to garnish

Soften the onion in the oil and margarine, without browning. Add the garlic, tomatoes, lemon juice and seasoning and stir well. Spoon one third of this sauce into a shallow ovenproof dish. Arrange the cod steaks on top and pour over the remaining sauce. Cover and bake in a moderately hot oven (190°C, 375°F, Gas Mark 5) for 25–30 minutes.

Strew with parsley just before serving.

Mackerel with Lemon and Bay Leaves

Per portion: 2800 kilojoules/670 calories
Serves 4 ♥

METRIC/IMPERIAL	AMERICAN
4 mackerel, cleaned and heads removed	4 mackerel, cleaned and heads removed
seasoned flour to toss	seasoned flour to toss
5 tablespoons polyunsaturated oil	6 tablespoons polyunsaturated oil
2 large Spanish onions, sliced	2 large Spanish onions, sliced
1 lemon, thinly sliced	1 lemon, thinly sliced
2 bay leaves, crumbled	2 bay leaves, crumbled
salt and freshly ground black pepper	salt and freshly ground black pepper

Toss the mackerel in the seasoned flour and fry on each side in the oil, until cooked through. Transfer to a heated serving dish and keep warm. Add the onions, lemon slices and bay leaves to the oil in the pan and cook gently until soft. Season to taste. Spoon over the fish and serve.

Mackerel must always be utterly fresh, with bright eyes and a sparkling silver body. Ask your fishmonger to clean the fish for you, and remove the heads.

Mackerel with Yogurt and Chives

A Norwegian dish.

Per portion: 2300 kilojoules/550 calories
Serves 4 ♥

METRIC/IMPERIAL	AMERICAN
4 mackerel, filleted	4 mackerel, filleted
2 tablespoons seasoned flour	3 tablespoons seasoned all-purpose flour
3 tablespoons polyunsaturated oil	¼ cup polyunsaturated oil
300 ml/½ pint natural low fat yogurt	1¼ cups plain low fat yogurt
3 tablespoons snipped chives	¼ cup snipped chives

Dust the mackerel fillets with the seasoned flour and fry on each side in the oil. Drain and discard the oil. Pour the mixed yogurt and chives over the fish and warm through gently, shuffling the pan, as the fish must not break or stick. Serve at once with plain boiled potatoes. As simple as it is delicious.

Psari Plaki

Bream baked in the oven. A Greek dish.

Per portion: 1135 kilojoules/315 calories
Serves 6 ♥

METRIC/IMPERIAL	AMERICAN
4 tablespoons polyunsaturated oil	⅓ cup polyunsaturated oil
2 onions, sliced	2 onions, sliced
0.5 kg/1 lb potatoes, sliced	1 lb potatoes, sliced
2 carrots, sliced	2 carrots, sliced
2 sticks celery, chopped	2 stalks celery, chopped
225 g/8 oz tomatoes, peeled and chopped	½ lb tomatoes, peeled and chopped
1 (1.5–1.75-kg/3–4-lb) bream	3–4 lb white fish
salt and freshly ground black pepper	salt and freshly ground black pepper
juice of 1 lemon	juice of 1 lemon
2 teaspoons chopped lemon thyme	2 teaspoons chopped lemon thyme
chopped parsley to garnish	chopped parsley to garnish

Heat the oil in a sauté pan and add the onions. Cook gently for a few moments then add the remaining vegetables in the order given. Cook, stirring occasionally, for about 10 minutes, until softened.

Lay the cleaned fish in a large oiled roasting dish. Sprinkle with salt and pepper and pour over the lemon juice. Scatter the chopped lemon thyme over the fish and surround with the vegetables. Pour the oil from the pan over the fish and the vegetables. Cover with foil and bake in a moderately hot oven (200°C, 400°F, Gas Mark 6) for 40–50 minutes, or until the fish is cooked, basting from time to time. Serve sprinkled with parsley.

Garlic and Tarragon Sauce for Steamed Fish

Total: 3490 kilojoules/860 calories
Makes 300 ml/½ pint (US: 1¼ cups)
♥

METRIC/IMPERIAL	AMERICAN
300 ml/½ pint dry white wine	1¼ cups dry white wine
3 sprigs tarragon	3 sprigs tarragon
50 g/2 oz polyunsaturated margarine	¼ cup polyunsaturated margarine
2 tablespoons flour	3 tablespoons all-purpose flour
1 clove garlic, crushed	1 clove garlic, crushed
150 ml/¼ pint chicken stock	⅔ cup chicken stock
salt and freshly ground black pepper	salt and freshly ground black pepper

To steam fish: place the skinned fillets (folded in three) on an oiled plate over a pan of boiling water. Invert another plate on top of the fish and cook over the steam for the required time. Meanwhile, make the sauce.

Reduce the wine by half, by fast boiling in an open pan. Add the chopped leaves of 2 tarragon sprigs and leave over a low heat until the scent of the herb is quite strong.

Melt the margarine and stir in the flour. Cook for 1 minute, then add the garlic, stock and seasoning. Bring to the boil, stirring all the time, until the sauce is smooth and thickened. Add the wine and tarragon mixture.

Just before serving, strain the sauce and add the remaining chopped tarragon leaves.

Plaice with Mushrooms and Cider

(illustrated opposite)

Per portion: 1720 kilojoules/420 calories
Serves 4 ♥

METRIC/IMPERIAL	AMERICAN
8 frozen plaice fillets	8 frozen flounder fillets
salt and white pepper	salt and white pepper
450 ml/¾ pint dry cider	2 cups dry cider
0.5 kg/1 lb button mushrooms	1 lb button mushrooms
1 tablespoon polyunsaturated oil	1 tablespoon polyunsaturated oil
50 g/2 oz polyunsaturated margarine	¼ cup polyunsaturated margarine
3 tablespoons flour	¼ cup all-purpose flour
450 g/1 lb potatoes, cooked	1 lb potatoes, cooked
parsley sprig to garnish	parsley sprig to garnish

Allow the fish fillets to thaw to room temperature. Season with salt and pepper, fold up each into three and lay in a sauté pan. Pour in the cider. Bring slowly to the boil. Cover and cook for 10 minutes over very gentle heat.

Meanwhile, slice the mushrooms and cook until just soft in the oil and margarine. Sprinkle on the flour and mix in carefully, until absorbed. Strain the cider liquor from the fish into a bowl and then add slowly to the mushrooms, stirring. Cook for a few minutes, stirring all the time, until the sauce thickens.

Arrange the plaice fillets on a hot serving dish and pour over the mushroom and cider sauce. Cream the potatoes with seasoning and skimmed milk, pipe a border around the fish, and brown under the grill. Garnish with a sprig of parsley and serve with a mixed green salad.

Trout with Almonds

A popular way of cooking trout in England and Scandinavia, where the lovely fresh fish is in need of no further adornment.

Per portion: 2800 kilojoules/670 calories
Serves 6 ♥

METRIC/IMPERIAL	AMERICAN
6 trout	6 trout
seasoned flour to toss	seasoned flour to toss
polyunsaturated oil to fry	polyunsaturated oil to fry
100 g/4 oz flaked almonds	1 cup flaked almonds
salt	salt
lemon wedges	lemon wedges

Clean the fish and remove the heads, or ask the fishmonger to do it for you. Toss the trout in seasoned flour. Heat just sufficient oil in a heavy-bottomed frying pan and add the fish. Cook for 3–4 minutes on each side, shuffling the pan to make sure the fish do not stick.

Meanwhile, gently fry the almonds in 2 tablespoons (US: 3 tablespoons) oil, until golden on both sides. Drain on to kitchen paper and sprinkle with salt.

Serve the trout scattered with the almonds and surrounded by lemon wedges.

Plaice with Mushrooms and Cider (see recipe above)

Kedgeree

Per portion: 2560 kilojoules/625 calories
Serves 4 ♥

METRIC/IMPERIAL	AMERICAN
0.5 kg/1 lb smoked haddock, soaked in cold water	1 lb smoked haddock, soaked in cold water
1 small onion, finely chopped	1 small onion, finely chopped
2 tablespoons polyunsaturated oil	3 tablespoons polyunsaturated oil
100 g/4 oz polyunsaturated margarine	$\frac{1}{2}$ cup polyunsaturated margarine
$\frac{1}{2}$ teaspoon curry powder	$\frac{1}{2}$ teaspoon curry powder
225 g/8 oz long-grain rice	1 cup long-grain rice
1 bay leaf	1 bay leaf
freshly ground black pepper	freshly ground black pepper
juice of 1 lemon	juice of 1 lemon
3 tablespoons chopped parsley	$\frac{1}{4}$ cup chopped parsley
lemon wedges to serve	lemon wedges to serve

Bring the haddock barely to the boil in fresh water, and simmer for a few minutes until tender. Drain and flake. Cook the onion in the oil and margarine until soft and golden. Sprinkle over the curry powder and cook for a minute longer.

Meanwhile, cook the rice in plenty of boiling salted water, with the bay leaf, for 10 minutes. Drain, and sprinkle over a few drops of cold water to separate the grains and stop the rice cooking. Combine the flaked haddock, the onion mixture and the rice. Grind plenty of black pepper into the kedgeree and sprinkle over the lemon juice and parsley. Toss lightly and pile into a hot dish.

Serve with lemon wedges.

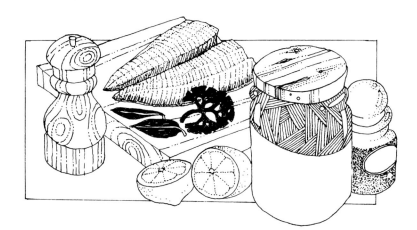

Salmon Parcels

The paper parcels puff up in the oven and release a succulent smell when opened on the plate.

Per portion: 2280 kilojoules/575 calories
Serves 4 ♥

METRIC/IMPERIAL	AMERICAN
75 g/3 oz fresh breadcrumbs	1$\frac{1}{2}$ cups fresh soft bread crumbs
100 g/4 oz polyunsaturated margarine	$\frac{1}{2}$ cup polyunsaturated margarine
1 teaspoon onion juice	1 teaspoon onion juice
rind and juice of 1 lemon	rind and juice of 1 lemon
4 tablespoons chopped parsley	$\frac{1}{3}$ cup chopped parsley
1 tablespoon chopped tarragon	1 tablespoon chopped tarragon
salt and freshly ground black pepper	salt and freshly ground black pepper
4 individual salmon steaks	4 individual salmon steaks
polyunsaturated oil	polyunsaturated oil
4 sheets greaseproof paper	4 sheets waxed paper

Fry the breadcrumbs lightly in the margarine until just absorbing the fat and barely colouring pale gold. Mix with the onion juice, grated lemon rind and juice, herbs and seasoning.

Place each salmon steak on a sheet of well-oiled greaseproof paper. Spoon the breadcrumb mixture on top and carefully do up the parcels so that none of the juices can escape. Place on a baking sheet and cook in a moderately hot oven (190°C, 375°F, Gas Mark 5) for 25–30 minutes.

Serve with plain boiled potatoes and a green vegetable or salad.

Fish Pie

Per portion: 1965 kilojoules/455 calories
Serves 6 ♥

METRIC/IMPERIAL	AMERICAN
0.75 kg/1½ lb cod or haddock fillets, or a mixture of white fish	1½ lb cod or haddock fillets, or a mixture of white fish
about 300 ml/½ pint skimmed milk	about 1¼ cups skimmed milk
1 bay leaf	1 bay leaf
½ onion, sliced	½ onion, sliced
6 peppercorns	6 peppercorns
75 g/3 oz polyunsaturated margarine	6 tablespoons polyunsaturated margarine
3 tablespoons flour	¼ cup all-purpose flour
salt and white pepper	salt and white pepper
2 tablespoons chopped parsley	3 tablespoons chopped parsley
4 tomatoes, peeled and sliced	4 tomatoes, peeled and sliced
1 kg/2 lb potatoes	2 lb potatoes
50 g/2 oz polyunsaturated margarine	¼ cup polyunsaturated margarine
150 ml/¼ pint hot skimmed milk	⅔ cup hot skimmed milk

Simmer the fish gently in milk and water to cover, with the bay leaf, onion and peppercorns, until cooked. Measure off the fish liquor and make up to 450 ml/¾ pint (US: 2 cups) with more skimmed milk if necessary.

Melt the margarine and stir in the flour. Cook over gentle heat for 1 minute then stir in the strained fish liquor. Bring to the boil, stirring all the time, until the sauce is smooth and thickened. Season to taste and stir in the chopped parsley. Pour a little of the sauce into a greased ovenproof dish, and lay the fish over it. Top with the tomato slices and cover with the remaining sauce.

Meanwhile, cook the potatoes and beat to a purée with half the margarine and the hot milk. Season and pile on top of the fish pie. Dot with the remaining margarine and brown under the grill for a few minutes. Keep warm in a low oven until ready to serve.

Green peas or a salad go well with this wholesome and popular family dish.

Meat

As the recipes in this section show, low cholesterol cooking can be as tasty, imaginative and varied as you choose to make it. Whether a roast leg of lamb, pork in wine sauce, veal with Marsala or a casserole of beef, see how to cook these and many others to your heart's content. Without the added richness of cream, butter or eggs, you will rise from the table feeling replete and content, but still as lively as a cricket.

Porc aux Pruneaux (see recipe page 36)

Porc aux Pruneaux

(illustrated on pages 34–35)

This is adapted from Curnonsky's 'Recettes des Provinces de France'. The dish is made up of pork fillet, the prunes that are so exquisitely displayed in the shop windows in Tours, and the delicious wine of the Loire, Vouvray, which comes from nearby.

Per portion: 2700 kilojoules/660 calories
Serves 4 ♥ ♥

METRIC/IMPERIAL	AMERICAN
0.5 kg/1 lb giant prunes	1 lb giant prunes
½ bottle Vouvray or medium dry white wine	½ bottle Vouvray or medium dry white wine
675 g/1½ lb pork fillet	1½ lb pork tenderloin
2 tablespoons seasoned flour	3 tablespoons seasoned all-purpose flour
1 tablespoon polyunsaturated oil	1 tablespoon polyunsaturated oil
50 g/2 oz polyunsaturated margarine	¼ cup polyunsaturated margarine
2 teaspoons redcurrant jelly	2 teaspoons red currant jelly
salt and freshly ground black pepper	salt and freshly ground black pepper
300 ml/½ pint natural low fat yogurt	1¼ cups plain low fat yogurt

Soak the prunes overnight in the wine.

Cut the pork fillet into cubes and turn in the seasoned flour. Fry gently on all sides in the oil and margarine until golden and cooked through.

Meanwhile, simmer the prunes for 30 minutes in the wine. Drain and place around the edge of a heated serving dish. Arrange the pork in the centre. Add the prune liquor to the meat juices in the frying pan, boil to reduce slightly and thicken, then stir in the redcurrant jelly until blended. Taste and adjust for seasoning. Carefully stir in half the yogurt and warm through. Pour over the pork, but not the prunes, and spoon over the remaining yogurt. Garnish with parsley and serve with a watercress and tomato salad.

Porc à l'Orange

Per portion: 1600 kilojoules/375 calories
Serves 6 ♥ ♥

METRIC/IMPERIAL	AMERICAN
1.25 kg/2½ lb pork fillet	2½ lb pork tenderloin
2 tablespoons seasoned flour	3 tablespoons seasoned all-purpose flour
2 tablespoons polyunsaturated oil	3 tablespoons polyunsaturated oil
little chopped rosemary	little chopped rosemary
450 ml/¾ pint light chicken stock	2 cups light chicken stock
juice of 2 oranges	juice of 2 oranges
juice of 1 lemon	juice of 1 lemon
2 tablespoons orange liqueur	3 tablespoons orange liqueur
2 tablespoons demerara sugar	3 tablespoons light brown sugar
salt and freshly ground black pepper	salt and freshly ground black pepper
orange slices to garnish	orange slices to garnish

Cut the pork fillet into small escalopes 2 cm/¾ inch (US: ¾ inch) thick, and toss in seasoned flour. Heat the oil in a large pan and gently fry the pork with the rosemary until tender. Transfer to a hot serving dish and keep warm.

Add the chicken stock to the meat juices in the pan, then stir in the fruit juices, liqueur and sugar. Bring to the boil, stirring, then simmer without a lid until reduced by half. Season, strain over the pork and garnish with orange slices.

Roast Lamb

Per 100 g/4 oz portion:
1200 kilojoules/330 calories
Serves 6 ♥ ♥ ♥

METRIC/IMPERIAL	AMERICAN
1 (1.5-kg/3-lb) leg of lamb	1 (3-lb) leg of lamb
3 tablespoons polyunsaturated oil	¼ cup polyunsaturated oil
2 tablespoons lemon juice	3 tablespoons lemon juice
2 cloves garlic, halved	2 cloves garlic, halved
1 sprig rosemary	1 sprig rosemary
salt and freshly ground black pepper	salt and freshly ground black pepper

Marinate the lamb in the oil and lemon juice for several hours, turning occasionally.

Place the garlic and rosemary in a roasting tin, add the lamb with the marinade and roast in a moderately hot oven (200°C, 400°F, Gas Mark 6) for 30 minutes. Baste. Reduce to moderate (180°C, 350°F, Gas Mark 4) for a further 1½ hours, basting from time to time. Transfer the lamb to a hot carving dish.

Carefully pour away all the fat from the roasting tin, and make a sauce by adding a little stock or wine to the juices in the pan. Strain and serve.

Navarin de Mouton

Per portion: 3770 kilojoules/900 calories
Serves 6 ♥ ♥ ♥

METRIC/IMPERIAL	AMERICAN
1.25 kg/2½ lb boned shoulder of lamb	2½ lb boned lamb shoulder
2 tablespoons polyunsaturated oil	3 tablespoons polyunsaturated oil
1 Spanish onion, chopped	1 Spanish onion, chopped
1 clove garlic, crushed	1 clove garlic, crushed
3 tablespoons flour	¼ cup all-purpose flour
salt and freshly ground black pepper	salt and freshly ground black pepper
300 ml/½ pint white wine	1¼ cups white wine
300 ml/½ pint light stock	1¼ cups light stock
6 baby carrots	6 baby carrots
6 baby turnips	6 baby turnips
12 tiny new potatoes	12 tiny new potatoes
12 button onions	12 button onions
225 g/8 oz shelled peas	½ lb peas, shelled weight
225 g/8 oz shelled broad beans	½ lb broad beans, shelled weight
chopped parsley to garnish	chopped parsley to garnish

Cut the lamb into 4-cm/1½-inch (US: 1½-inch) cubes and trim away any excess fat. Heat the oil in a large flameproof casserole and use to brown the lamb, onion and garlic. Sprinkle over the flour and seasoning and mix until it is all absorbed. Gradually blend in the wine and stock and bring to the boil. Cover and simmer gently for 1 hour. Allow to become cold and skim off any fat from the surface.

Now add the vegetables to the lamb, peeled or scraped as necessary: carrots, turnips, potatoes, onions, peas and beans. Return to simmering point, cover and cook gently for a further 30 minutes. Serve sprinkled with chopped parsley.

Saltimbocca

Per portion: 4050 kilojoules/490 calories
Serves 4 ♥ ♥ ♥

METRIC/IMPERIAL	AMERICAN
8 slices raw smoked ham	8 slices raw smoked ham
8 small sage leaves	8 small sage leaves
8 thin slices veal fillet	8 thin slices veal fillet
flour to coat	flour to coat
1 tablespoon polyunsaturated oil	1 tablespoon polyunsaturated oil
50 g/2 oz polyunsaturated margarine	¼ cup polyunsaturated margarine
150 ml/¼ pint Marsala or white wine	⅔ cup Marsala or white wine
twist of lemon peel	twist of lemon peel
salt and freshly ground black pepper	salt and freshly ground black pepper

Place a slice of ham and a sage leaf on each veal fillet. Roll up and tie with cotton. Coat the rolls lightly with flour.

Heat the oil and margarine in a frying pan. Put in the veal olives and cook on all sides until they start to turn golden. Pour in the Marsala or wine and add the lemon peel. Simmer gently for about 10 minutes, season to taste, and serve on a hot dish with the sauce spooned over.

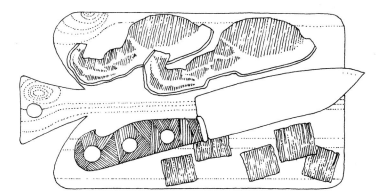

Italian Veal Casserole

(illustrated opposite)

Per portion: 1315 kilojoules/315 calories
Serves 6 ♥ ♥ ♥

METRIC/IMPERIAL	AMERICAN
6 slices shin of veal (each 5 cm/2 inches thick), or 0.75 kg/1½ lb pie veal	6 slices shin of veal (each 2 inches thick), or 1½ lb pie veal
3 tablespoons polyunsaturated oil	¼ cup polyunsaturated oil
seasoned flour to coat	seasoned flour to coat
150 ml/¼ pint dry white wine	⅔ cup dry white wine
1 Spanish onion, finely chopped	1 Spanish onion, finely chopped
0.75 kg/1½ lb tomatoes, peeled and roughly chopped	1½ lb tomatoes, peeled and roughly chopped
1 teaspoon chopped lemon thyme	1 teaspoon chopped lemon thyme
½ teaspoon dried oregano	½ teaspoon dried oregano
150 ml/¼ pint light stock	⅔ cup light stock
salt and freshly ground black pepper	salt and freshly ground black pepper
1 lemon	1 lemon
2 cloves garlic, crushed (optional)	2 cloves garlic, crushed (optional)
2 tablespoons chopped parsley	3 tablespoons chopped parsley

Shin of veal is the traditional flavoursome cut used for this dish. If using pie veal, trim and cube.

Heat the oil in a heavy-bottomed flameproof casserole. Cook the veal, lightly dusted with the seasoned flour, until golden. If using shin, stand the veal upright, so the marrow does not fall out of the bone. Add the wine, onion, tomatoes, herbs, stock and seasoning. Bring to simmering point, cover and cook gently for 1½–2 hours. Take off the lid after the first hour if the sauce needs reducing.

Grate the rind of the lemon and mix with the garlic and parsley. Sprinkle over the casserole just before serving. Italian risotto rice, coloured with a pinch of saffron, goes well with this marvellous dish.

Spaghetti alla Marinara

Taught to my husband by a Tuscan sailor. Very good.

Per portion: 3170 kilojoules/755 calories
Serves 4 ♥ ♥

METRIC/IMPERIAL	AMERICAN
350 g/12 oz spaghetti	3 cups spaghetti
2 Spanish onions, chopped	2 Spanish onions, chopped
3 tablespoons polyunsaturated oil	¼ cup polyunsaturated oil
1 tablespoon finely chopped rosemary	1 tablespoon finely chopped rosemary
2 cloves garlic, crushed	2 cloves garlic, crushed
1 (793-g/1 lb 12-oz) can tomatoes	1 (1 lb 12-oz) can tomatoes
5 tablespoons tomato purée	½ cup tomato paste
salt and freshly ground black pepper	salt and freshly ground black pepper
½ teaspoon sugar	½ teaspoon sugar
0.5 kg/1 lb lean minced beef	1 lb lean ground beef

Cook the spaghetti for 10 minutes in plenty of fast boiling salted water. Drain, toss in oil or margarine and grind over plenty of black pepper.

Meanwhile, cook the onions in the oil until soft but not brown. Add the rosemary and garlic and fry gently for a little longer. Stir in the tomatoes, tomato purée, salt, pepper and sugar. Simmer, uncovered, for 10–15 minutes. Mix in the beef and stir until all the grains are separate. Bring gently back to the boil and simmer for 3 minutes only. Serve immediately, piled on the spaghetti.
Note: The beef *must* be good quality and freshly minced.

Italian Veal Casserole (see recipe above)

Moussaka

Per portion: 1965 kilojoules/465 calories
Serves 6 ♥ ♥ ♥

METRIC/IMPERIAL	AMERICAN
0.5 kg/1 lb aubergines, sliced	1 lb eggplants, sliced
polyunsaturated oil to fry	polyunsaturated oil to fry
1 onion, chopped	1 onion, chopped
2 cloves garlic, crushed	2 cloves garlic, crushed
$\frac{1}{2}$ teaspoon dried oregano or marjoram	$\frac{1}{2}$ teaspoon dried oregano or marjoram
2 tomatoes, peeled and chopped	2 tomatoes, peeled and chopped
0.75 kg/1$\frac{1}{2}$ lb minced lamb or beef	1$\frac{1}{2}$ lb ground lamb or beef
150 ml/$\frac{1}{4}$ pint red wine	$\frac{2}{3}$ cup red wine
bouquet garni	bouquet garni
salt and freshly ground black pepper	salt and freshly ground black pepper
300 ml/$\frac{1}{2}$ pint tomato sauce (see page 61)	1$\frac{1}{4}$ cups tomato sauce (see page 61)
300 ml/$\frac{1}{2}$ pint béchamel sauce (see page 61)	1$\frac{1}{4}$ cups béchamel sauce (see page 61)
75 g/3 oz low-fat cheese, grated (Edam or Gouda)	$\frac{3}{4}$ cup grated low-fat cheese (Edam or Gouda)

Sprinkle the aubergines liberally with salt and leave to drain in a colander for an hour. Rinse and pat dry with kitchen paper. Heat just sufficient oil in a large frying pan and use to fry the aubergine slices on both sides. Drain on kitchen paper.

Now make the meat sauce. Fry the onion, garlic and oregano in a little oil until soft. Add the tomatoes, meat and red wine. Stir with a wooden spoon until the grains of meat are separate. Add the bouquet garni and barely simmer, uncovered, for about 15 minutes. Season to taste.

Make up the tomato and béchamel sauces.

Now assemble in a large and shallow greased ovenproof dish. Begin with the meat sauce then layer the tomato sauce, aubergine slices and béchamel sauce. Finally sprinkle over the grated cheese. Cook in a moderate oven (180°C, 350°F, Gas Mark 4) for 45 minutes.

A salad is all you need serve with this satisfying and substantial Greek dish.

Old English Casserole of Beef

Per portion: 2165 kilojoules/520 calories
Serves 6 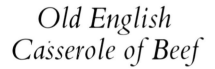 ♥ ♥ ♥

METRIC/IMPERIAL	AMERICAN
1 kg/2 lb shin of beef	2 lb shin of beef
flour to toss	flour to toss
4 large carrots	4 large carrots,
3 tablespoons polyunsaturated oil	$\frac{1}{4}$ cup polyunsaturated oil
24 shallots	24 shallots
1 tablespoon dry mustard	1 tablespoon dry mustard
1 teaspoon dried mixed herbs	1 teaspoon dried mixed herbs
450 ml/$\frac{3}{4}$ pint beef stock	2 cups beef stock
salt and freshly ground black pepper	salt and freshly ground black pepper
1 tablespoon grated horseradish	1 tablespoon grated horseradish
2 tablespoons brandy	3 tablespoons brandy

Trim any fat and gristle from the beef and cut the meat into 2-cm/$\frac{3}{4}$-inch (US: $\frac{3}{4}$-inch) cubes. Toss in the flour. Roughly chop the carrots.

Heat the oil in a large casserole and brown the meat rapidly on all sides. Take out and set aside. Add the carrots and shallots to the pan and cook for a few minutes over a low heat, stirring with a wooden spoon. When the vegetables are golden, remove and put with the meat. Sprinkle the mustard and herbs onto the remaining oil and pan juices and stir well. Gradually blend in the stock. Return the meat and vegetables to the pan and add seasoning to taste. Heat through and cover tightly.

Cook in a moderate oven (160°C, 325°F, Gas Mark 3) for 2–3 hours, until the meat is tender. You may need to reduce the heat still further after the first hour. Just before serving, stir in the horseradish and brandy.

Roast Beef Fillet

Per complete portion:
2085 kilojoules/500 calories
Serves 6 ♥ ♥ ♥

METRIC/IMPERIAL
0.75 kg/1½ lb potatoes
chopped rosemary
polyunsaturated oil and margarine
1.25 kg/2½ lb fillet of beef
150 ml/¼ pint red wine
For the horseradish sauce
2 tablespoons grated horseradish
grated rind and juice of ½ lemon
50 g/2 oz walnuts, chopped
150 ml/¼ pint natural low fat yogurt

AMERICAN
1½ lb potatoes
chopped rosemary
polyunsaturated oil and margarine
2½ lb fillet of beef
⅔ cup red wine
For the horseradish sauce
3 tablespoons grated horseradish
grated rind and juice of ½ lemon
½ cup chopped walnuts
⅔ cup plain low fat yogurt

Cut the peeled potatoes into small chunks and cook for 4 minutes in boiling salted water. Drain and pat dry. Sprinkle with rosemary and roast in oil and margarine in a moderately hot oven (200°C, 400°F, Gas Mark 6) for 50 minutes.

Brush the meat with oil and set on a grid in a roasting tin. Roast in the oven below the potatoes, allowing 40–50 minutes, according to taste. After 20 minutes, drain any fat from the tin. Heat the wine, pour over the meat and continue cooking, basting occasionally.

Mix together the ingredients for the horseradish sauce. Pile the potatoes in a small dish. Carve the beef on to a heated serving dish, strain over the juices from the roasting tin and serve with the horseradish sauce.

Spinach makes an excellent accompaniment to this dish.

Casserole of Beef with Wine

Per portion: 1875 kilojoules/450 calories
Serves 6 ♥ ♥ ♥

METRIC/IMPERIAL
1 kg/2 lb lean braising steak
2 tablespoons polyunsaturated oil
2 large onions, chopped
2 cloves garlic, crushed
50 g/2 oz lean smoked bacon, diced
2 tablespoons flour
salt and freshly ground black pepper
½ teaspoon dried oregano
300 ml/½ pint dry red wine
5 tablespoons tomato purée, diluted in a
little water

AMERICAN
2 lb lean chuck beef
3 tablespoons polyunsaturated oil
2 large onions, chopped
2 cloves garlic, crushed
2 slices Canadian bacon, diced
3 tablespoons all-purpose flour
salt and freshly ground black pepper
½ teaspoon dried oregano
1¼ cups dry red wine
½ cup tomato paste, diluted in a little
water

Cut the beef into 4-cm/1½-inch (US: 1½-inch) cubes. Heat the oil in a large, thick-bottomed casserole and fry the onion and garlic until golden. Add the bacon and cook for a few minutes. Stir in the flour and then add the beef, combining all well together. Season lightly and add the remaining ingredients. Cover and bring slowly back to the boil.

Transfer to a cool oven (150°C, 300°F, Gas Mark 3) for 2 hours, until tender. Reduce the heat after 1 hour if the casserole is cooking faster than a very gentle bubbling. Adjust for seasoning and serve from the casserole.

Poultry and Game

Chicken is deservedly popular these days, as it can be used to make such a range of good dishes: flambéed with red wine and brandy; grilled with a barbecue sauce; in a delicious wine and cheese sauce; or simply roast, in the very best manner. Rabbit with mustard, duckling with a rich port and olive sauce, and turkey cooked in a way that tastes nothing like Christmas, all add to this selection of very special poultry and game recipes.

Chicken en Cocotte (see recipe page 44)

Chicken en Cocotte

(illustrated on pages 42–43)

Per portion: 2850 kilojoules/715 calories
Serves 4 ♥

METRIC/IMPERIAL
1 (1.5-kg/3–3½-lb) chicken, jointed
salt and freshly ground black pepper
2 tablespoons polyunsaturated oil
50 g/2 oz polyunsaturated margarine
50 g/2 oz lean smoked ham, diced
4 small onions, chopped
1 clove garlic, crushed
2 tablespoons brandy
6 tomatoes, peeled and chopped
3 carrots, chopped
2 sticks celery, cut into 4-cm/1½-inch
lengths
¼ teaspoon chopped thyme
1 bay leaf
300 ml/½ pint red wine
chopped parsley to garnish
(optional)

AMERICAN
1 (3–3½-lb) chicken, jointed
salt and freshly ground black pepper
3 tablespoons polyunsaturated oil
¼ cup polyunsaturated margarine
¼ cup diced lean smoked ham
4 small onions, chopped
1 clove garlic, crushed
3 tablespoons brandy
6 tomatoes, peeled and chopped
3 carrots, chopped
2 stalks celery, cut into 1½-inch
lengths
¼ teaspoon chopped thyme
1 bay leaf
1¼ cups red wine
chopped parsley to garnish
(optional)

Season the chicken portions with salt and pepper. Melt the oil and margarine in a casserole or flambé pan and add the diced ham and chicken portions. Cook until golden, turning. Take out the meats and set aside.

Fry the onions and garlic in the pan fat until softened, stirring. Return the chicken and ham to the pan. Pour on the brandy and flambé the meats. Now add the tomatoes, carrots, celery, thyme, bay leaf and red wine. Bring to the boil, cover and simmer for about 30 minutes, until the chicken and vegetables are tender. Remove the bay leaf before serving and sprinkle with chopped parsley.

Chicken with White Wine and Tarragon

Per portion: 2065 kilojoules/505 calories
Serves 6 ♥ ♥

METRIC/IMPERIAL
1 (1.5–1.75-kg/3½–4-lb) chicken,
with giblets
2 tablespoons polyunsaturated oil
salt and freshly ground black pepper
twist of lemon peel
sprig tarragon
300 ml/½ pint water
50 g/2 oz polyunsaturated margarine
2 tablespoons flour
150 ml/¼ pint dry white wine
2 teaspoons Dijon mustard
2 tablespoons chopped tarragon
(or ½ teaspoon dried)
75 g/3 oz Gouda cheese, grated

AMERICAN
1 (3½–4-lb) chicken,
with giblets
3 tablespoons polyunsaturated oil
salt and freshly ground black pepper
twist of lemon peel
sprig tarragon
1¼ cups water
¼ cup polyunsaturated margarine
3 tablespoons all-purpose flour
⅔ cup dry white wine
2 teaspoons Dijon mustard
3 tablespoons chopped tarragon
(or ½ teaspoon dried)
¾ cup grated Gouda cheese

Brush the bird all over with oil and sprinkle with salt and pepper. Tuck the twist of lemon peel and sprig of tarragon inside the chicken. Place in a roasting tin, pour in the water and arrange the giblets around the bird. Cover the tin loosely with foil or greaseproof paper. Cook in a moderately hot oven (200°C, 400°F, Gas Mark 6) for 1¼–1½ hours, until cooked. Take up the chicken and joint and carve it. Lay the pieces on a hot dish and cover with the foil or greaseproof paper. Keep warm while you make the sauce.

Melt the margarine in a saucepan. Stir in the flour and cook for 1 minute. Gradually stir in the strained juices from the roasting tin, then add the white wine. Bring to the boil, stirring constantly, and flavour with the mustard and tarragon. Stir in the grated cheese. Simmer, stirring, for a few minutes. Pour over the chicken and serve immediately.

Stuffed Pot-Roasted Chicken

Per portion: 1890 kilojoules/460 calories
Serves 6 ♥

METRIC/IMPERIAL	AMERICAN
100 g/4 oz long-grain rice	½ cup long-grain rice
1 (1.75-kg/4-lb) chicken, with giblets	1 (4-lb) chicken, with giblets
2 tablespoons polyunsaturated oil	3 tablespoons polyunsaturated oil
50 g/2 oz raisins	⅓ cup raisins
1 small green pepper, deseeded and chopped	1 small green pepper, deseeded and chopped
grated rind of 1 lemon	grated rind of 1 lemon
salt and freshly ground black pepper	salt and freshly ground black pepper
0.5 kg/1 lb onions, quartered	1 lb onions, quartered
0.5 kg/1 lb baby carrots	1 lb baby carrots
0.5 kg/1 lb small tomatoes, peeled and quartered	1 lb small tomatoes, peeled and quartered
¼ teaspoon chopped rosemary	¼ teaspoon chopped rosemary
300 ml/½ pint dry cider	1¼ cups dry cider
little lemon juice	little lemon juice

Cook the rice in boiling salted water for 10 minutes, until just tender. Drain well. Chop the chicken liver roughly and cook for a few minutes in a little of the oil. Mix together the cooked rice, chicken liver, raisins, green pepper, grated lemon rind and seasoning. Stuff the chicken with this mixture.

Grease a casserole dish large enough to take the chicken comfortably. Place the onions, carrots and tomatoes in the bottom, and lay the chicken on top. Brush the chicken with the remaining oil and sprinkle on the rosemary. Pour the cider around the chicken.

Cover the casserole and cook in a moderate oven (180°C, 350°F, Gas Mark 4) for 2 hours, until the chicken is tender. Remove the lid for the last 10 minutes to brown the bird.

Lift out the chicken and place on a hot serving dish. Remove the vegetables carefully with a slotted spoon and arrange around the bird. Strain the juices from the casserole into a small pan and add a squeeze of lemon juice. Reheat and serve separately in a jug or sauceboat.

This needs only plain boiled potatoes tossed in a little polyunsaturated margarine and some finely chopped parsley. Follow with a crisp green salad. Simply delicious.

Grilled Devilled Chicken

Per portion: 2085 kilojoules/500 calories
Serves 4 ♥

METRIC/IMPERIAL	AMERICAN
1 (1.5-kg/3½-lb) chicken, jointed, or 4 chicken portions	1 (3½-lb) chicken, jointed, or 4 chicken portions
1 tablespoon French mustard	1 tablespoon French mustard
1 teaspoon ground ginger	1 teaspoon ground ginger
1 teaspoon salt	1 teaspoon salt
1 teaspoon freshly ground black pepper	1 teaspoon freshly ground black pepper
1 teaspoon Worcestershire sauce	1 teaspoon Worcestershire sauce
½ teaspoon sugar	½ teaspoon sugar
juice of 1 lemon	juice of 1 lemon
4 tablespoons polyunsaturated oil	⅓ cup polyunsaturated oil

Place the chicken portions in a shallow ovenproof dish. Mix together the mustard, ginger, salt, pepper, Worcestershire sauce, sugar and lemon juice. Use to coat the chicken portions and leave to marinate for several hours, turning occasionally in the marinade.

Sprinkle the oil over the chicken portions and place under a preheated grill, not too close, starting with the skin side uppermost. Allow 15–20 minutes on each side, although cooking time may be shorter if you do this on an outside barbecue.

Serve with a green salad and rice pilaf (see page 53).

Roast Chicken with Tarragon

This is the very best way to roast a chicken, as it part steams, part roasts, and this preserves the juices and delicious flavour.

Per portion: 2125 kilojoules/510 calories
Serves 4 ♥

METRIC/IMPERIAL
1 (1.5-kg/3–3½-lb) roasting chicken, with giblets
75 g/3 oz polyunsaturated margarine
salt and freshly ground black pepper
chopped tarragon, fresh or dried
twist of lemon peel
300 ml/½ pint hot water
cornflour to thicken
white wine or lemon juice (see method)

AMERICAN
1 (3–3½-lb) roasting chicken, with giblets
6 tablespoons polyunsaturated margarine
salt and freshly ground black pepper
chopped tarragon, fresh or dried
twist of lemon peel
1¼ cups hot water
cornstarch to thicken
white wine or lemon juice (see method)

Remove the giblets from the chicken. Sprinkle a small knob of the margarine with salt, pepper and tarragon and pop inside the chicken with the twist of lemon peel. Brush the chicken generously with the remaining margarine, melted, and scatter tarragon overall. Season the bird lightly. Place in a roasting tin with the giblets, and pour in the hot water. Cover the tin loosely with foil, and cook in a moderately hot oven (200°C, 400°F, Gas Mark 6) for about 1¼ hours. Check occasionally during cooking that the liquid in the tin has not dried out – add a little more water if it looks low.

When the chicken is ready the leg joints should move freely, and when pierced with a fine skewer the juice that runs should be clear, not pink. Lift the bird on to a hot carving dish, remove the giblets and turn your attention to the beautiful juices left in the pan. Thicken them with a little cornflour, moistened in cold water, then add a dash of white wine, or a squeeze of lemon juice, according to taste. Strain and serve.

Duckling with Olives

(illustrated opposite)

Per average portion:
2035 kilojoules/555 calories
Serves 4–6 ♥

METRIC/IMPERIAL
1 (2-kg/4½-lb) young duck, with giblets
salt
2 carrots, diced
2 sticks celery, finely chopped
mushroom stalks (optional)
bouquet garni
300 ml/½ pint cider
175 g/6 oz Spanish stuffed green olives
50 g/2 oz polyunsaturated margarine
2 tablespoons flour
150 ml/¼ pint port

AMERICAN
1 (4½-lb) young duck, with giblets
salt
2 carrots, diced
2 stalks celery, finely chopped
mushroom stalks (optional)
bouquet garni
1¼ cups cider
1 cup Spanish stuffed green olives
¼ cup polyunsaturated margarine
3 tablespoons all-purpose flour
⅔ cup port

Remove the giblets from the duck and reserve. Prick the duck with a sharp fork, particularly around the fatty areas at the top of the legs. Sprinkle with salt, place on a rack in a roasting tin and cook in a hot oven (220°C, 425°F, Gas Mark 7) for 30 minutes. Take out the duck, remove the rack and pour away all the fat. Return the duck to the roasting tin. Arrange the giblets around it with the carrots, celery, mushroom stalks, bouquet garni and cider. Place a piece of foil loosely over the duck and return the roasting tin to a moderately hot oven (190°C, 375°F, Gas Mark 5) for 1 hour, until the duck is cooked through and tender. Remove the foil for the last 10 minutes to crisp the skin.

Blanch the olives in gently boiling water for 5 minutes. Melt the margarine, stir in the flour and cook for 1 minute. Gradually stir in the port and bring to the boil, stirring, until the sauce is smooth and thickened.

Place the duck on a hot serving dish. Surround with two-thirds of the strained olives. Cover with foil and keep warm. Pour away any fat from the roasting tin, carefully strain the juices remaining in the tin through a sieve and add them to the sauce with the remaining olives. Heat through the sauce and serve separately. Garnish the duck with a twist of orange, olive and watercress, and serve with an orange and watercress salad.

Duckling with Olives (see recipe above)

Civet de Lièvre

Per portion: 2000 kilojoules/500 calories
Serves 8 ♥ ♥

METRIC/IMPERIAL	AMERICAN
1 hare, jointed	1 hare, jointed
2 tablespoons polyunsaturated oil	3 tablespoons polyunsaturated oil
100 g/4 oz smoked bacon, trimmed of fat and diced	6 slices bacon, trimmed of fat and diced
12 button onions	12 button onions
2 tablespoons flour	3 tablespoons all-purpose flour
24 chestnuts, peeled (see page 82)	24 chestnuts, peeled (see page 82)
2 teaspoons redcurrant jelly	2 teaspoons red currant jelly
3 small squares dark chocolate, grated	1 square semisweet chocolate, grated
For the marinade	*For the marinade*
1 onion, chopped	1 onion, chopped
1 carrot, chopped	1 carrot, chopped
4 tablespoons polyunsaturated oil	$\frac{1}{3}$ cup polyunsaturated oil
$\frac{3}{4}$–1 bottle red wine	$\frac{3}{4}$–1 bottle red wine
salt and freshly ground black pepper	salt and freshly ground black pepper
bouquet garni	bouquet garni
2 cloves garlic, crushed	2 cloves garlic, crushed

The hare should be adequately hung and carefully jointed by your butcher. It will need to be marinated for a day or two, so plan well ahead.

To prepare the marinade, cook the onion and carrot for a few minutes in the oil, then add the remaining ingredients. Pour over the hare portions in a deep casserole. Cover, and turn the meat occasionally. Marinate for 1–2 days.

When you are ready to cook the dish, remove the hare portions and lay on a plate. Keep the marinade in a bowl by the cooker. Rinse and dry the casserole.

Heat the oil in the casserole and use to brown the bacon and button onions. Take out the onions and reserve. Sprinkle the flour over the bacon and stir. Put in the hare portions, pour over the marinade, stirring to incorporate, and bring gently to the boil. Barely simmer, covered, for 1½–2 hours. 30 minutes before the end of the cooking time, add the button onions, chestnuts, redcurrant jelly and grated chocolate.

Remove the hare portions, the button onions and the chestnuts and place on a large hot serving dish. Reduce the sauce if necessary (boil rapidly, stirring, without a lid) and then strain over the meat.

Hand redcurrant jelly separately and serve with puréed potatoes and a fresh green vegetable.

Polly's Lapin à la Moutarde

This is a recipe from a friend on the island of Ibiza.

Per portion: 1670 kilojoules/400 calories
Serves 4 ♥ ♥

METRIC/IMPERIAL	AMERICAN
3 tablespoons Dijon mustard	$\frac{1}{4}$ cup Dijon mustard
2 tablespoons fresh breadcrumbs	3 tablespoons fresh soft bread crumbs
2 tablespoons polyunsaturated oil	3 tablespoons polyunsaturated oil
1 young rabbit	1 young rabbit
1 heaped tablespoon cornflour	1 heaped tablespoon cornstarch
300 ml/½ pint white wine or cider	1¼ cups white wine or cider
salt and freshly ground black pepper	salt and freshly ground black pepper
2 tablespoons natural low fat yogurt	3 tablespoons plain low fat yogurt

Mix together the mustard, breadcrumbs and oil.

Coat the rabbit with this mixture, place in a roasting tin and cook in a moderately hot oven (200°C, 400°F, Gas Mark 6) for 50 minutes, or until tender. Lift the rabbit on to a hot carving dish and keep warm.

Mix the cornflour with a little cold water and pour into the roasting tin with the white wine. Cook gently on top of the cooker for a few minutes, stirring with a wooden spoon. Season, remove from the heat and stir in the yogurt. Strain into a warm sauceboat and serve with the rabbit.

Turkey in Vermouth

Per average portion:
1590 kilojoules/420 calories
Serves 6 ♥

METRIC/IMPERIAL	AMERICAN
1 (3–3.5-kg/7–8-lb) turkey	1 (7–8-lb) turkey
3 tablespoons polyunsaturated oil	¼ cup polyunsaturated oil
1 tablespoon chopped tarragon	1 tablespoon chopped tarragon
1 small onion, chopped	1 small onion, chopped
2 sticks celery, chopped	2 stalks celery, chopped
4 medium carrots, chopped	4 medium carrots, chopped
300 ml/½ pint dry white vermouth	1¼ cups dry white vermouth
For the stuffing	*For the stuffing*
75 g/3 oz fresh white breadcrumbs	1½ cups fresh soft white bread crumbs
100 g/4 oz polyunsaturated margarine, melted	½ cup polyunsaturated margarine, melted
grated rind of 1½ lemons	grated rind of 1½ lemons
4 tablespoons chopped parsley	⅓ cup chopped parsley
½ teaspoon chopped thyme	½ teaspoon chopped thyme
salt and freshly ground black pepper	salt and freshly ground black pepper
100 g/4 oz green grapes, halved and pipped	¼ lb white grapes, halved and pipped

Mix together the stuffing ingredients and spoon into the bird. Brush the turkey all over with oil and sprinkle with the chopped tarragon. Lay the onion, celery and carrots in the base of a large oblong casserole dish or roasting tin. Place the turkey on the bed of vegetables and pour around the vermouth. Cover and cook in a moderately hot oven (190°C, 375°F, Gas Mark 5) for about 2½–3 hours. Baste from time to time with the pan juices. Add a little hot giblet stock or water, if necessary, to keep the dish moist.

The turkey will be succulent and tender. Slice the flesh, and serve with a spoonful of stuffing and the juices from the casserole, strained.

Paprika Chicken

Per portion: 2915 kilojoules/695 calories
Serves 4 ♥

METRIC/IMPERIAL	AMERICAN
1 (1.5-kg/3-lb) chicken	1 (3-lb) chicken
2 tablespoons polyunsaturated oil	3 tablespoons polyunsaturated oil
3 tablespoons chopped tarragon (or 1 teaspoon dried)	¼ cup chopped tarragon (or 1 teaspoon dried)
300 ml/½ pint giblet stock	1¼ cups giblet stock
For the sauce	*For the sauce*
1 tablespoon polyunsaturated oil	1 tablespoon polyunsaturated oil
25 g/1 oz polyunsaturated margarine	2 tablespoons polyunsaturated margarine
1 onion, finely chopped	1 onion, finely chopped
1 clove garlic, crushed	1 clove garlic, crushed
2 teaspoons paprika pepper	2 teaspoons paprika pepper
2 tablespoons flour	3 tablespoons all-purpose flour
225 g/8 oz tomatoes, peeled and chopped	½ lb tomatoes, peeled and chopped
300 ml/½ pint white wine or cider	1¼ cups white wine or cider
2 caps tinned pimiento, chopped	2 caps tinned pimiento, chopped
salt and freshly ground black pepper	salt and freshly ground black pepper
150 ml/¼ pint natural low fat yogurt	⅔ cup plain low fat yogurt

Brush the chicken with the oil and sprinkle the tarragon inside and out. Stand in a roasting tin, pour around the giblet stock, cover loosely with greaseproof paper or foil and cook in a moderately hot oven (200°C, 400°F, Gas Mark 6) for 1¼ hours.

Meanwhile, prepare the sauce. Heat the oil and margarine and use to cook the onion and garlic until quite soft. Sprinkle on the paprika and flour and mix in well. Add the tomatoes, white wine or cider, chopped pimiento and seasoning. Bring to the boil, stirring constantly, and simmer until well reduced. Just before serving, remove from the heat and stir in the yogurt.

Joint or carve the cooked chicken on to a hot dish and pour over the sauce. Serve with noodles tossed in margarine and sprinkled with chopped parsley.

Vegetable Dishes and Salads

As some of the more exotic vegetables become
widely available, so has vegetable cooking
become more imaginative and unusual; try
a casserole of aubergines with cottage cheese,
Jerusalem artichokes with tomatoes and garlic,
or that constant French favourite, ratatouille.
Salads are no longer simply summer fare; many
winter vegetables are delicious used raw to make
crisp, crunchy salads, especially with the
addition of some chopped nuts or fruit, all
tossed in a piquant dressing.

Red Cabbage (see recipe page 52)

Red Cabbage

(illustrated on pages 50–51)

Good with winter and Christmas dishes.

Per portion: 660 kilojoules/165 calories
Serves 6 ♥

METRIC/IMPERIAL	AMERICAN
1 kg/2 lb red cabbage	2 lb red cabbage
50 g/2 oz polyunsaturated margarine	¼ cup polyunsaturated margarine
1 tablespoon polyunsaturated oil	1 tablespoon polyunsaturated oil
1 onion, chopped	1 onion, chopped
2 crisp green apples, peeled and chopped	2 crisp green apples, peeled and chopped
1 teaspoon caraway seeds	1 teaspoon caraway seeds
1 teaspoon salt	1 teaspoon salt
freshly ground black pepper	freshly ground black pepper
2 tablespoons demerara sugar	3 tablespoons light brown sugar
5 tablespoons red wine vinegar	6 tablespoons red wine vinegar
5 tablespoons water	6 tablespoons water

Cut the cabbage in half lengthways and remove the thick white stalk. Shred finely.

Melt the margarine and oil in a large, heavy-based pan. Add the cabbage, onion, apples and remaining ingredients. Stir well, bring up to boiling point then cover and cook gently for 50–60 minutes, stirring from time to time, until the cabbage is tender.

Braised Fennel

Celery can be treated in the same way. Serve as a first course, or as a vegetable with fish and meat dishes.

Per portion: 200 kilojoules/45 calories
Serves 4 ♥

METRIC/IMPERIAL	AMERICAN
2 bulbs fennel	2 bulbs fennel
300 ml/½ pint stock	1¼ cups stock
15 g/½ oz polyunsaturated margarine	1 tablespoon polyunsaturated margarine

Trim and rinse the fennel. Cut each bulb in half and blanch in boiling salted water for 5 minutes. Drain thoroughly.

Place the fennel in a shallow ovenproof dish, pour over the stock and dot with margarine. Cover the dish with a lid or foil and cook in a moderately hot oven (190°C, 375°F, Gas Mark 5) for 20–30 minutes, until tender.

Aubergine Casserole

Per portion: 595 kilojoules/140 calories
Serves 6 ♥

METRIC/IMPERIAL	AMERICAN
3–4 medium aubergines, sliced	3–4 medium eggplants, sliced
salt and freshly ground black pepper	salt and freshly ground black pepper
polyunsaturated oil to fry	polyunsaturated oil to fry
225 g/8 oz cottage cheese	1 cup cottage cheese
8 tomatoes, peeled and sliced	8 tomatoes, peeled and sliced
4 tablespoons fresh breadcrumbs	⅓ cup fresh soft bread crumbs
1 clove garlic, crushed	1 clove garlic, crushed

Sprinkle the aubergine slices liberally with salt and leave to drain in a colander for about 1 hour. This removes any bitterness. Rinse and pat dry, then fry in oil until golden brown on both sides. Drain on kitchen paper.

Lightly oil a deep ovenproof dish, place a layer of aubergine slices in the bottom, season and cover with cottage cheese. Season again and cover with a layer of tomato slices. Repeat the layers until the ingredients are used up, then top with the breadcrumbs lightly fried in oil and garlic. Cook in a moderately hot oven (190°C, 375°F, Gas Mark 5) for 40–45 minutes.

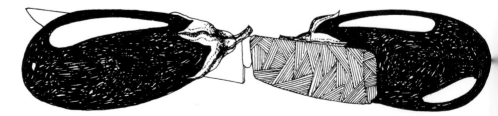

Topinambours Provençale

Per portion : 305 kilojoules/70 calories
Serves 6 ♥

METRIC/IMPERIAL	AMERICAN
1 kg/2 lb Jerusalem artichokes, scraped	2 lb Jerusalem artichokes, scraped
2 large cloves garlic, crushed	2 large cloves garlic, crushed
1 tablespoon polyunsaturated oil	1 tablespoon polyunsaturated oil
0.5 kg/1 lb tomatoes, peeled, deseeded and chopped	1 lb tomatoes, peeled, deseeded and chopped
2 tablespoons tomato purée	3 tablespoons tomato paste
juice of ½ lemon	juice of ½ lemon
1 tablespoon chopped basil (or ½ teaspoon dried basil)	1 tablespoon chopped basil (or ½ teaspoon dried basil)
1 teaspoon sugar	1 teaspoon sugar
salt and freshly ground black pepper	salt and freshly ground black pepper
2 tablespoons chopped parsley	3 tablespoons chopped parsley

Slice the artichokes thickly and steam or poach until tender, about 20 minutes.

Meanwhile, warm the garlic in the oil, add the tomatoes and cook for about 10 minutes, stirring frequently, until the liquid has reduced a little. When the texture is pulpy, add the tomato purée, lemon juice, basil, sugar and seasoning. Heat through and pour over the cooked artichokes in a serving dish. Just before serving sprinkle with chopped parsley. This is equally delicious served hot or cold.

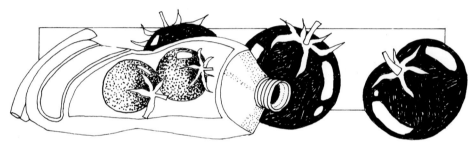

Rice Pilaf

Per portion : 1390 kilojoules/335 calories
Serves 4 ♥

METRIC/IMPERIAL	AMERICAN
225 g/8 oz long-grain rice	1 cup long-grain rice
1 onion, chopped	1 onion, chopped
2 tablespoons polyunsaturated oil	3 tablespoons polyunsaturated oil
1 teaspoon ground turmeric	1 teaspoon ground turmeric
1 tablespoon currants	1 tablespoon currants
1 (226-g/8-oz) can pineapple pieces, drained	1 (8-oz) can pineapple pieces, drained

Cook the rice in boiling salted water for 10 minutes. Drain and sprinkle with a little cold water to separate the grains. Keep warm in a covered dish.

Fry the onion in the oil, add the turmeric, currants and pineapple pieces. Toss the rice in this mixture and serve.

Courgettes

Per portion : 735 kilojoules/175 calories
Serves 4 ♥

METRIC/IMPERIAL	AMERICAN
0.75 kg/1½ lb courgettes, sliced	1½ lb zucchini, sliced
4 tablespoons polyunsaturated oil	⅓ cup polyunsaturated oil
1 clove garlic, crushed	1 clove garlic, crushed
juice of ½ lemon	juice of ½ lemon
freshly ground black pepper	freshly ground black pepper
sea salt	sea salt
chopped parsley to garnish	chopped parsley to garnish

Fry the courgettes in oil with the garlic, lemon juice and pepper, turning once, until they are soft and golden brown. Season with salt, sprinkle over parsley and serve.

Add some peeled, deseeded and roughly chopped tomatoes to the courgettes to make Courgettes Provençale.

Riced Potatoes

♥

Plain boiled potatoes are made into a lovely light snow by an old-fashioned gadget, obtainable from most caterers' suppliers and some kitchen shops, called simply a potato ricer.

Use the ricer for cooked swedes as well. Mix the riced swedes with a little crushed garlic, and season well with sea salt and freshly ground black pepper. Toss in a generous amount of polyunsaturated margarine. Not a bit like school veg!

French Beans and Mushrooms Vinaigrette

(illustrated opposite)

Per portion: 850 kilojoules/205 calories
Serves 8 ♥

METRIC/IMPERIAL	AMERICAN
1 kg/2 lb frozen whole French beans	2 lb frozen whole green beans
0.5 kg/1 lb button mushrooms	1 lb button mushrooms
juice of ½ lemon	juice of ½ lemon
½ small onion, grated	½ small onion, grated
little ground coriander	little ground coriander
3 tablespoons chopped parsley	¼ cup chopped parsley
250 ml/scant ½ pint French dressing	1 cup French dressing
(see page 60)	(see page 60)

Cook the beans in boiling salted water until just tender, then cool under running water. Drain thoroughly.

Wipe the mushrooms with a clean damp cloth and slice finely. Sprinkle with lemon juice. Add the onion, coriander and parsley to the French dressing, then pour over the mushrooms. Turn gently for an hour or two.

Toss the mushroom mixture carefully with the French beans and serve in a simple china dish.

Ratatouille

This can also be served as a starter, either hot or cold, depending on the rest of the meal and the state of the weather. Assemble the ingredients, prepare them in the order given below, and the cooking times will be just right. You will need a large, heavy sauté pan with a lid.

Per portion: 975 kilojoules/235 calories
Serves 6 ♥

METRIC/IMPERIAL	AMERICAN
2 aubergines, cubed	2 eggplants, cubed
2 large Spanish onions, sliced	2 large Spanish onions, sliced
6 tablespoons polyunsaturated oil	½ cup polyunsaturated oil
2 cloves garlic, crushed	2 cloves garlic, crushed
3 green peppers, deseeded and diced	3 green peppers, deseeded and diced
4 courgettes, sliced	4 zucchini, sliced
8 ripe tomatoes, peeled and chopped	8 ripe tomatoes, peeled and chopped
½ teaspoon dried thyme	½ teaspoon dried thyme
1 teaspoon dried oregano	1 teaspoon dried oregano
salt and freshly ground black pepper	salt and freshly ground black pepper
1 teaspoon sugar	1 teaspoon sugar

Place the aubergines in a colander, sprinkle with salt and leave to drain for 30 minutes. Rinse and pat dry.

Soften the onions in the oil, and then add the vegetables as you prepare them, turning well with each addition. Add the aubergines at the same time as the courgettes. Toss in the herbs, seasoning and sugar, cover and cook gently for a further 20–30 minutes, stirring from time to time.

Serve hot sprinkled with chopped parsley, or cold on a bed of lettuce leaves, garnished with black olives.

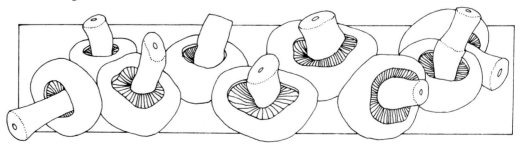

54

French Beans and Mushrooms Vinaigrette (see recipe above)

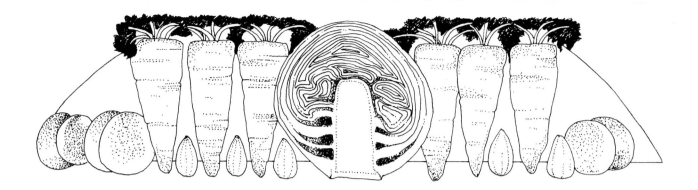

Obbie's Salad

Per portion: 1615 kilojoules/385 calories
Serves 6 ♥

METRIC/IMPERIAL
75 g/3 oz blanched halved almonds
polyunsaturated oil to fry
salt to toss
½ small white cabbage, finely
shredded
225 g/8 oz carrot, grated, marinated in
fresh orange juice
1 lettuce, shredded
3 Kabanos sausages, sliced
3 peaches
150 ml/¼ pint French dressing
(see page 60)

AMERICAN
¾ cup blanched halved almonds
polyunsaturated oil to fry
salt to toss
½ small head white cabbage, finely
shredded
generous 2 cups grated carrot, marinated
in fresh orange juice
1 lettuce, shredded
3 Kabanos sausages, sliced
3 peaches
⅔ cup French dressing
(see page 60)

Fry the almonds in oil and toss quickly in salt while still hot.

Assemble the cabbage, carrot, lettuce and sausage slices in a large bowl. Just before serving, peel and slice the peaches and add to the salad with the French dressing and almonds. Toss all together and serve.

Note: Kabanos sausages can be bought at delicatessen counters.

Carrot Salad

Per portion: 310 kilojoules/80 calories
Serves 4 ♥

METRIC/IMPERIAL
0.5 kg/1 lb carrots, grated
juice of 2 oranges
2 tablespoons raisins
salt and freshly ground black pepper

AMERICAN
1 lb carrots, grated
juice of 2 oranges
3 tablespoons raisins
salt and freshly ground black pepper

Simply toss all together.

Coleslaw

Per portion: 1050 kilojoules/250 calories
Serves 8 ♥

METRIC/IMPERIAL
1 small white cabbage
4 Cox's apples
juice of 1 lemon
1 head celery
50 g/2 oz walnuts, chopped
2 tablespoons chopped parsley
2 tablespoons snipped chives
1 green pepper, deseeded and chopped
250 ml/scant ½ pint French dressing
(see page 60)

AMERICAN
1 small head white cabbage
4 dessert apples
juice of 1 lemon
1 bunch celery
½ cup chopped walnuts
3 tablespoons chopped parsley
3 tablespoons snipped chives
1 green pepper, deseeded and chopped
1 cup French dressing
(see page 60)

Shred the cabbage finely, discarding the tough white stalk. Core and chop the apples (leaving the skin on) and toss in the lemon juice. Wash and chop the celery, using the tender inside leaves and stalks. Place the cabbage, apples, celery and remaining ingredients in a large bowl. Pour over enough French dressing to coat and toss all together well.

Rice Salad

Per portion: 1705 kilojoules/410 calories
Serves 8 ♥

METRIC/IMPERIAL	AMERICAN
450 g/1 lb long-grain rice	1 lb long-grain rice
1 (184-g/6½-oz) can pimientos, rinsed and chopped	1 (6½-oz) can pimientos, rinsed and chopped
1 (340-g/12-oz) can sweetcorn, drained	1 (12-oz) can corn, drained
1 teaspoon chopped lemon thyme	1 teaspoon chopped lemon thyme
2 tablespoons chopped parsley	3 tablespoons chopped parsley
250 ml/scant ½ pint French dressing (see page 60)	1 cup French dressing (see page 60)

Cook the rice in boiling salted water for 10 minutes. Drain and sprinkle with cold water to separate the grains. Combine with the remaining ingredients and pour over enough French dressing to moisten. Toss well together and cool.

Avocado Pear Salad

Per portion: 535 kilojoules/125 calories
Serves 6 ♥

METRIC/IMPERIAL	AMERICAN
3 avocado pears	3 avocados
juice of 1 lemon	juice of 1 lemon
1 lettuce, washed and shredded	1 lettuce, washed and shredded
sea salt and freshly ground black pepper	sea salt and freshly ground black pepper

Halve, peel and slice the avocados lengthways. Sprinkle with the lemon juice and arrange on a bed of lettuce leaves. Tuck the avocado stones into the dish until the last minute (this prevents the pears from browning) and cover with cling film.

To serve, uncover, remove the stones and season with salt and freshly ground black pepper.

Peach and Ginger Salad

This is good as a starter, as well as an accompaniment to cold meats.

Per portion: 625 kilojoules/150 calories
Serves 4 ♥

METRIC/IMPERIAL	AMERICAN
3 peaches	3 peaches
juice of ½ lemon	juice of ½ lemon
2 tablespoons sliced preserved ginger	3 tablespoons sliced preserved ginger
1 lettuce heart	1 lettuce heart
3 tablespoons French dressing (see page 60)	¼ cup French dressing (see page 60)
chopped parsley to garnish	chopped parsley to garnish

Scald the peaches by plunging into a bowl of boiling water for 1 minute. Skin and slice and sprinkle with lemon juice. Mix with the sliced ginger and arrange on a bed of lettuce. Spoon over the French dressing and scatter with parsley.

Sauces and Basic Recipes

All together in one useful section are those recipes that form every cook's standby, and which are referred to constantly; the basic sauces, and some sauces for special occasions, two delicious pastries – one made with polyunsaturated margarine, one with corn oil – recipes for homemade yogurt, curd cheese and salad dressings, plus a basic pancake batter – always useful to make a quick and tasty supper dish, served with a savoury filling or sweet sauce.

Mayonnaise (see recipe page 60)
French Dressing (see recipe page 60)

59

French Dressing

(illustrated on pages 58–59)

Total: 5560 kilojoules/1330 calories
Per tablespoon: 330 kilojoules/80 calories
Makes 250 ml/scant ½ pint
(US: 1 cup) dressing ♥

METRIC/IMPERIAL	AMERICAN
4 tablespoons wine vinegar	⅓ cup wine vinegar
150 ml/¼ pint pure corn oil	⅔ cup pure corn oil
1 teaspoon castor sugar	1 teaspoon sugar
1 teaspoon salt	1 teaspoon salt
1 teaspoon freshly ground black pepper	1 teaspoon freshly ground black pepper
1 clove garlic, crushed (optional)	1 clove garlic, crushed (optional)

Measure all the ingredients into a screw-topped jar (preferably non-metallic as metal corrodes). Shake up well before using and store in the refrigerator. The quantity can be increased as long as the ratio of one part vinegar to two parts oil is kept. Shake before using.

Mayonnaise

(illustrated on pages 58–59)

Total: 12130 kilojoules/2710 calories
Per tablespoon:
470 kilojoules/100 calories
Makes generous 300 ml/½ pint
(US: 1¼ cups) ♥

METRIC/IMPERIAL	AMERICAN
1 egg	1 egg
½ teaspoon dry mustard	½ teaspoon dry mustard
½ teaspoon salt	½ teaspoon salt
¼ teaspoon sugar	¼ teaspoon sugar
1½ tablespoons vinegar	2 tablespoons vinegar
300 ml/½ pint pure corn oil	1¼ cups pure corn oil

Break the egg into the goblet of the liquidiser. Add mustard, salt, sugar and vinegar. Turn on at a low speed and add half the oil in a very small stream through the lid, stopping every few seconds to let the egg take up and emulsify the oil. The remaining oil can be poured in quite steadily.

Homemade mayonnaise can be made with lemon juice instead of vinegar, and sweetened with a little honey. It can be flavoured with the addition of chives, parsley, herbs, garlic, capers, olives or gherkins, finely chopped. Stored in a covered container, it will keep for up to a week in the refrigerator.

This contains the yolk of one egg, but of course each serving will only have a fraction of it.

Cumberland Sauce

To serve with Christmas ham, game and cold meats, or to make as a gift.

Total: 4200 kilojoules/1000 calories
Serves 8 ♥

METRIC/IMPERIAL	AMERICAN
1 small onion, finely chopped	1 small onion, finely chopped
2 oranges	2 oranges
1 lemon	1 lemon
1 (227-g/8-oz) jar redcurrant jelly	1 (8-oz) jar red currant jelly
1 teaspoon Dijon mustard	1 teaspoon Dijon mustard
150 ml/¼ pint port	⅔ cup port
2 teaspoons cornflour, mixed with 1 tablespoon cold water	2 teaspoons cornstarch, mixed with 1 tablespoon cold water

Put the chopped onion in a small saucepan. Pare the rind of 1 orange and the lemon with a potato peeler, cut into very thin strips and add to the onion. Cover with cold water, bring to the boil and cook for 5 minutes. Drain and throw away the water.

Put the redcurrant jelly in a bowl over a saucepan of boiling water. Stir the jelly until melted. Push through a sieve to remove any lumps, if necessary, then return to the bowl over simmering water. Stir in the mustard, port, the juice of both oranges and the lemon, the blanched rind and onion. Cook for 5 minutes then stir in the moistened cornflour. Simmer for a further 2–3 minutes, stirring, then pour into a jar and leave to cool.

Seal tightly and leave for a week before using. This will keep for about two months, but should be stored in the refrigerator once opened.

Béchamel Sauce

Total: 4440 kilojoules/1120 calories
Makes 600 ml/1 pint
(US: 2½ cups) ♥

METRIC/IMPERIAL	AMERICAN
2 tablespoons polyunsaturated oil	3 tablespoons polyunsaturated oil
50 g/2 oz polyunsaturated margarine	¼ cup polyunsaturated margarine
40 g/1½ oz flour	⅓ cup all-purpose flour
600 ml/1 pint skimmed milk	2½ cups skimmed milk
salt and white pepper	salt and white pepper
1 bay leaf (optional)	1 bay leaf (optional)

Melt the oil and margarine in a saucepan and blend in the flour. Cook for 1 minute. Add a little of the milk and when it bubbles, beat with a wooden spoon until smooth. Continue adding the rest of the milk like this. Season to taste and cook gently for at least 5 minutes, stirring constantly. Infuse the bay leaf in this, if liked, to give a stronger flavour to the sauce.

Velouté Sauce

Total: 1920 kilojoules/470 calories
Makes 600 ml/1 pint
(US: 2½ cups) ♥

METRIC/IMPERIAL	AMERICAN
50 g/2 oz polyunsaturated margarine	¼ cup polyunsaturated margarine
40 g/1½ oz flour	⅓ cup all-purpose flour
600 ml/1 pint chicken or veal stock	2½ cups chicken or veal stock
salt and white pepper	salt and white pepper

Melt the margarine and stir in the flour to form a roux. Heat the stock to boiling and add to the roux a little at a time, stirring vigorously with a wooden spoon or whisk. The sauce should cook for at least 6–7 minutes, stirring constantly, and be the thickness of runny cream. Season to taste and strain through a sieve before serving.
Note: Fish velouté is made in the same way, using fish stock.

Tomato Sauce

Total: 2180 kilojoules/520 calories
Makes about 600 ml/1 pint
(US: 2½ cups) ♥

METRIC/IMPERIAL	AMERICAN
1 Spanish onion, chopped	1 Spanish onion, chopped
2 tablespoons polyunsaturated oil	3 tablespoons polyunsaturated oil
1 clove garlic, crushed	1 clove garlic, crushed
½ teaspoon dried oregano	½ teaspoon dried oregano
1 (793-g/1 lb 12-oz) can tomatoes	1 (1 lb 12-oz) can tomatoes
5 tablespoons tomato purée	½ cup tomato paste
1 teaspoon sugar	1 teaspoon sugar
1 teaspoon salt	1 teaspoon salt
freshly ground black pepper	freshly ground black pepper
1 bay leaf	1 bay leaf
twist of lemon peel	twist of lemon peel

Soften the onion in the oil without browning. Add the remaining ingredients and bring to the boil, stirring. Cover and simmer for 15 minutes. Remove the lemon peel and bay leaf and adjust the seasoning.

Cranberry Sauce

Total: 1350 kilojoules/330 calories
Serves 6 ♥

METRIC/IMPERIAL	AMERICAN
175 g/6 oz cranberries	1½ cups cranberries
150 ml/¼ pint water	⅔ cup water
2 tablespoons demerara sugar	3 tablespoons light brown sugar
little grated orange rind	little grated orange rind
2 tablespoons brandy	3 tablespoons brandy

Place all the ingredients in a saucepan. Cook over gentle heat, stirring, until the cranberries pop and burst. Serve hot, in a sauceboat, to accompany roast turkey.

Shortcrust Pastry

Total: 8320 kilojoules/1930 calories
Makes 225 g/8 oz
(US: ½ lb) dough ♥

METRIC/IMPERIAL	AMERICAN
150 g/5 oz polyunsaturated margarine	½ cup plus 2 tablespoons polyunsaturated margarine
225 g/8 oz plain flour, sifted	2 cups all-purpose flour, sifted
2 tablespoons water	3 tablespoons water

Place the margarine, one-third of the flour and the water in a mixing bowl and mix together with a fork until well combined. Stir in the remaining flour and mix to a dough. Turn out on to a lightly floured board and knead lightly until smooth. Kneading improves this pastry dough.

Easy Mix Pastry with Oil

Total: 5910 kilojoules/1400 calories
Makes 175 g/6 oz
(US: 6 oz) dough ♥

METRIC/IMPERIAL	AMERICAN
5 tablespoons pure corn oil	6 tablespoons pure corn oil
3 tablespoons water	scant ¼ cup water
175 g/6 oz plain flour (or use self-raising flour for a lighter, crumblier texture)	1½ cups all-purpose flour (sifted with 1½ teaspoons baking powder for a lighter, crumblier texture)
½ teaspoon salt	½ teaspoon salt

Whisk together the oil and water and pour all at once on to the sifted flour and salt. Mix with a fork, combine, then knead lightly to a manageable dough, which leaves the sides of the bowl clean.

Roll out immediately, thinly, between sheets of greaseproof paper, without extra flour. The easiest way to use the pastry is to peel off the top paper and place the crust in position with the paper side up; peel off.

Pancake Batter

Per pancake: 450 kilojoules/115 calories
Makes about 8 ♥

METRIC/IMPERIAL	AMERICAN
100 g/4 oz plain flour	1 cup all-purpose flour
½ teaspoon salt	½ teaspoon salt
2 teaspoons castor sugar (for sweet batters only)	2 teaspoons castor sugar (for sweet batters only)
1 egg	1 egg
1 tablespoon polyunsaturated oil	1 tablespoon polyunsaturated oil
300 ml/½ pint skimmed milk	1¼ cups skimmed milk
polyunsaturated oil for frying	polyunsaturated oil for frying

Sift the flour, salt and sugar in a large bowl. Mix the egg, oil and milk and add slowly to the dry ingredients. Beat well and then set aside for 1 hour. The batter should be like runny cream; add more milk if necessary.

Place a medium-sized frying pan on top of the cooker and heat gently. Rub the base of the hot pan with kitchen paper dipped in oil, and pour in just enough batter to coat the bottom. When tiny bubbles appear in the pancake, lift up the edges and peep underneath; if it is golden toss the pancake in the air to turn and cook the other side.

The pancakes can be stacked and kept warm, or reheated, over a pan of boiling water.

Pizza Quiche (see recipe page 14)

Homemade Yogurt

*Per 150 ml/¼ pint (US: ⅔ cup): 235 kilojoules/60 calories
Makes 750 ml/1¼ pints (US: 3 cups)* ♥

METRIC/IMPERIAL	AMERICAN
150 ml/5 fl oz natural unsweetened low fat yogurt	⅔ cup plain unsweetened low fat yogurt
600 ml/1 pint skimmed milk, made up using 100 g/4 oz skimmed milk powder	2½ cups skimmed milk made up using 1⅓ cups skimmed milk powder

Mix together in a bowl, cover and leave in a warm place, such as the airing cupboard, for 4–6 hours, or until set (depending on the warmth). Stir once, and chill in the refrigerator. Save some at the end to make up the next batch of yogurt.

It is marvellous for breakfast with fresh fruit and muesli, will add to soups and sauces, makes a delicious sweet with puréed or whole fruits and can be eaten on its own with a spoonful of honey or soft brown sugar. It is so convenient to always keep a bowl of yogurt in the refrigerator; I wish I could sell it to you strongly enough!

Soft Curd Cheese

*Total: 3350 kilojoules/800 calories
Makes 225 g/8 oz (US: ½ lb)* ♥

METRIC/IMPERIAL	AMERICAN
2.25 litres/4 pints skimmed milk	5 pints skimmed milk
300 ml/½ pint natural low fat yogurt	1¼ cups plain low fat yogurt
1 tablespoon rennet	1 tablespoon rennet

Sterilise all equipment before beginning.

Heat the milk to blood heat and add the yogurt and rennet. Pour into a clear bowl, cover and leave in a warm place to set (8–10 hours). Strain off the whey, put the curd into a muslin or fine cotton bag and strain again (a colander or sieve is ideal for this purpose). Leave for 1 hour and then replace with fresh muslin. Allow to drip again until the dripping stops (approximately 2 hours). Replace with fresh muslin and chill in the refrigerator before using.

This can be used in cooking or eaten just as it is; it is most useful to thicken a sauce that might otherwise call for egg yolks or cream; substituted for cream cheese in recipes; eaten with bread, biscuits or oatcakes; very good mixed with a little garlic and fresh herbs; or shaped into a ball and rolled in finely chopped parsley, or coarsely ground black pepper.

Cucumber and Mint Sauce

*Total: 790 kilojoules/190 calories
Makes 450 ml/¾ pint (US: 2 cups)* ♥

METRIC/IMPERIAL	AMERICAN
½ cucumber, thinly sliced	½ cucumber, thinly sliced
1½ teaspoons salt	1½ teaspoons salt
300 ml/½ pint natural low fat yogurt	1¼ cups plain low fat yogurt
2 tablespoons chopped mint	3 tablespoons chopped mint
salt and pepper	salt and pepper

Sprinkle the cucumber with the salt and leave to drain for an hour in a colander. Press gently to drain off any surplus juice. Turn the cucumber into a bowl, and stir in the yogurt and mint. Season to taste.

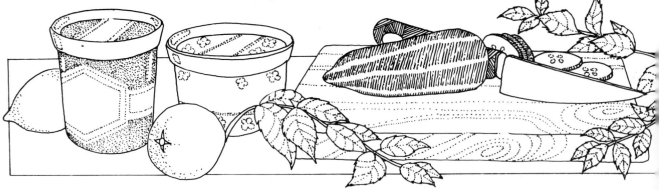

Low Cholesterol Soured Cream

Total: 1170 kilojoules/280 calories
Makes 150 ml/¼ pint (US: ⅔ cup) ♥

METRIC/IMPERIAL	AMERICAN
2 tablespoons skimmed milk	3 tablespoons skimmed milk
1 tablespoon lemon juice	1 tablespoon lemon juice
225 g/8 oz low fat cottage cheese	1 cup low fat cottage cheese
¼ teaspoon salt	¼ teaspoon salt

Measure the ingredients into a liquidiser in the order listed above. Cover and blend for 30 seconds or until smooth. Chill.

Snipped chives are excellent stirred into this, to accompany meat or fish, or to top a baked jacket potato. Or serve as a dressing for salad, or as a sauce for a mousse with the addition of some freshly chopped tarragon or dill. If using in a hot dish, add at the last moment.

Cucumber Sauce

Excellent with mackerel or cold salmon.

Total: 1400 kilojoules/330 calories
Makes 150 ml/¼ pint (US: ⅔ cup) ♥

METRIC/IMPERIAL	AMERICAN
½ cucumber, peeled, deseeded and chopped	½ cucumber, peeled, deseeded and chopped
salt	salt
225 g/8 oz cottage cheese, sieved	1 cup cottage cheese, sieved
2 tablespoons natural low fat yogurt	3 tablespoons plain low fat yogurt
2 tablespoons chopped mint	3 tablespoons chopped mint
white pepper	white pepper

Salt the cucumber lightly and drain in a colander for 15 minutes. Blend the cucumber and cottage cheese in the liquidiser with enough yogurt to bring the sauce to the consistency of thick cream. Stir in the mint and season to taste.

Brandy Butter

Per portion: 1085 kilojoules/275 calories
Serves 8 ♥

METRIC/IMPERIAL	AMERICAN
225 g/8 oz castor sugar	1 cup sugar
100 g/4 oz polyunsaturated margarine	½ cup polyunsaturated margarine
150 ml/¼ pint brandy	⅔ cup brandy
1 teaspoon lemon juice	1 teaspoon lemon juice
grated rind of 1 orange	grated rind of 1 orange

Beat the sugar and margarine together until light and fluffy. Beat in the brandy, a little at a time, then the lemon juice. Add the grated orange rind, cover and chill until required.

Just
Desserts

Once you have begun to try out these desserts,
you will wonder why you ever needed eggs or
cream. Use fresh fruit in season, or
the simplest of ingredients, to make the perfect
dessert every time; peaches in brandy, apricot
yogurt, pancakes with orange and lemon sauce,
lime, lemon or blackcurrant sorbet – all full of
flavour, light and refreshing.

Compote of Rhubarb (see recipe page 68)
Gooseberry Fool with Brandy Snaps (see recipe page 68)
Geranium Creams (see recipe page 68)

Geranium Creams

(illustrated on pages 66–67)

Per portion: 1100 kilojoules/265 calories
Serves 3 ♥

METRIC/IMPERIAL	AMERICAN
225 g/8 oz cottage cheese	1 cup cottage cheese
2 tablespoons natural low fat yogurt	3 tablespoons plain low fat yogurt
3 tablespoons castor sugar	$\frac{1}{4}$ cup sugar
scented geranium leaves	scented geranium leaves
1 tablespoon castor sugar	1 tablespoon sugar
fruit in season	fruit in season

Blend the cottage cheese, yogurt and 3 tablespoons (US: $\frac{1}{4}$ cup) sugar together in the liquidiser. Spoon into individual heart-shaped moulds, lined with cheesecloth, cover with a scented geranium leaf and leave on a dish to drain overnight.

Turn out, if liked, on to a bed of freshly picked and prettily arranged geranium leaves. Sprinkle over the remaining sugar and serve with the fruit.
Note: Tiny wild strawberries, when in season, are delicious with the geranium creams.

Compote of Rhubarb

(illustrated on pages 66–67)

Per portion: 395 kilojoules/105 calories
Serves 6 ♥

METRIC/IMPERIAL	AMERICAN
1 kg/2 lb rhubarb	2 lb rhubarb
100 g/4 oz sugar, or to taste	$\frac{1}{2}$ cup sugar, or to taste
1 sugar cube	1 sugar cube
1 orange	1 orange
1 tablespoon chopped preserved ginger	1 tablespoon chopped preserved ginger
curls of orange peel to decorate	curls of orange peel to decorate
(optional)	(optional)

Wash and cut the rhubarb into 5-cm/2-inch (US: 2-inch) lengths. Barely cook the rhubarb over very low heat with sugar to taste.

Rub the sugar cube over the orange, to become impregnated with the zest. Crush the sugar cube and add to the rhubarb with the chopped ginger. Chill.

This looks pretty served in a white china dish with curls of orange peel (use your potato peeler) to decorate. Hand a bowl of homemade yogurt separately, and a dish of dark brown sugar.

Gooseberry Fool with Brandy Snaps

(illustrated on pages 66–67)

Per portion fool: 670 kilojoules/160 calories
Serves 4 ♥

METRIC/IMPERIAL	AMERICAN
0.5 kg/1 lb gooseberries	1 lb gooseberries
75 g/3 oz sugar	6 tablespoons sugar
450 ml/$\frac{3}{4}$ pint natural low fat yogurt	2 cups plain low fat yogurt
brandy snaps (see page 77)	brandy snaps (see page 77)
dark soft brown sugar	dark brown sugar

Rinse the gooseberries and drain well. Cook gently with the sugar in a covered pan until the sugar has dissolved and the fruit is soft. Add a little water if the fruit looks like sticking to the pan. Push the pulp through a fine sieve. Cool, then fold in the yogurt. Serve with brandy snaps and a bowl of dark brown sugar.

Apricot Yogurt

Per portion: 905 kilojoules/215 calories
Serves 6 ♥

METRIC/IMPERIAL	AMERICAN
225 g/8 oz dried apricots	$\frac{1}{2}$ lb dried apricots
150 g/5 oz castor sugar	$\frac{2}{3}$ cup sugar
600 ml/1 pint natural low fat yogurt	2$\frac{1}{2}$ cups plain low fat yogurt

Soak the apricots overnight, in water to cover, then cook gently for about 30 minutes, until tender. Blend in the liquidiser with a little of the cooking liquid, or press through a sieve. Add the sugar and stir well to dissolve. Cool and mix into the yogurt. Serve in individual china pots.

Peaches in Brandy

Per portion: 950 kilojoules/225 calories
Serves 6 ♥

METRIC/IMPERIAL	AMERICAN
175 g/6 oz castor sugar	¾ cup sugar
600 ml/1 pint water	2½ cups water
12 peaches	12 peaches
juice of 1½ lemons	juice of 1½ lemons
4 tablespoons brandy	⅓ cup brandy

Dissolve the sugar in the water, stirring, until it reaches boiling point. Boil for 6 minutes and then cool.

Pour boiling water over the peaches. Leave for 1 minute then plunge into cold water. Peel carefully, halve and remove the stones. Arrange in a beautiful glass bowl and sprinkle with the lemon juice. Add the brandy to the cooled sugar syrup and pour over the peaches. Cover with cling film and chill until required.

Serve with a pile of baby meringues (see page 77).

Danish Apple Charlotte

Per portion: 1310 kilojoules/320 calories
Serves 4 ♥

METRIC/IMPERIAL	AMERICAN
50 g/2 oz fresh white breadcrumbs	1 cup fresh soft white bread crumbs
75 g/3 oz sugar	6 tablespoons sugar
1 tablespoon polyunsaturated oil	1 tablespoon polyunsaturated oil
25 g/1 oz polyunsaturated margarine	2 tablespoons polyunsaturated margarine
¼ teaspoon ground cinnamon	¼ teaspoon ground cinnamon
0.75 kg/1½ lb cooking apples, peeled cored and sliced	1½ lb baking apples, peeled, cored and sliced
100 g/4 oz raspberry jam, warmed	¼ lb raspberry jam, warmed

Mix the breadcrumbs with one third of the sugar and fry until golden in the oil and margarine. Sprinkle with the cinnamon.

Cook the apples gently with the remaining sugar in a lidded saucepan until soft. Stir occasionally to prevent sticking. Beat to a purée.

Fill a glass dish with alternate layers of crumbs, apple purée and raspberry jam, beginning and ending with a layer of crumbs. Cool and serve with a bowl of homemade yogurt (see page 64).

Fresh Orange Jelly

Per portion: 700 kilojoules/180 calories
Serves 4 ♥

METRIC/IMPERIAL	AMERICAN
4 sugar cubes	4 sugar cubes
4 oranges	4 oranges
75 g/3 oz castor sugar	6 tablespoons sugar
300 ml/½ pint water	1¼ cups water
20 g/¾ oz gelatine	3 envelopes gelatin
juice of 1 lemon	juice of 1 lemon
2 oranges, segmented	2 oranges, segmented

Rub each sugar cube over an orange until it has absorbed as much flavour as possible. Crush. Squeeze the juice from the oranges.

Put the crushed sugar, castor sugar, water and gelatine in a saucepan and stir over gentle heat until dissolved. Cool slightly and add the strained juice of the oranges and lemon. Pour half this jelly mixture into individual glass dishes and chill the refrigerator until set. Keep the remaining jelly in a warmer place. When the jelly has set in the glasses, top with the fresh orange segments and pour over the rest of the jelly. Replace in the refrigerator.

This makes a refreshingly different sweet, and one especially popular with children.

Pancakes St Clements

Per portion: 1440 kilojoules/365 calories
Serves 4 ♥

METRIC/IMPERIAL
8 cooked pancakes (see page 62)
For the sauce
1 orange, shredded, pips discarded
½ lemon, shredded, pips discarded
75 g/3 oz castor sugar
1 tablespoon water
2 teaspoons cornflour
2 tablespoons orange liqueur

AMERICAN
8 cooked pancakes (see page 62)
For the sauce
1 orange, shredded, pips discarded
½ lemon, shredded, pips discarded
6 tablespoons sugar
1 tablespoon water
2 teaspoons cornstarch
3 tablespoons orange liqueur

Simmer the orange, lemon, sugar and water in a covered pan for about 30 minutes, stirring occasionally. Do not allow the fruit to stick; add a little more water if necessary. Just before serving, moisten the cornflour with a little cold water and stir in enough to thicken the sauce slightly. Finally add the liqueur and heat through. Serve in a sauceboat to pour over the hot pancakes.

Cherry and Almond Meringue

(illustrated opposite)

Per portion: 1830 kilojoules/455 calories
Serves 6 ♥

METRIC/IMPERIAL
For the pastry
175 g/6 oz flour
75 g/3 oz polyunsaturated margarine
2 tablespoons cold water
grated rind of 1 lemon
1 teaspoon castor sugar
pinch salt
For the filling
0.5 kg/1 lb ripe black cherries
175 g/6 oz castor sugar
1 tablespoon lemon juice
75 g/3 oz ground almonds
2 large egg whites

AMERICAN
For the pastry
1½ cups all-purpose flour
6 tablespoons polyunsaturated margarine
3 tablespoons cold water
grated rind of 1 lemon
1 teaspoon sugar
pinch salt
For the filling
1 lb ripe bing cherries
¾ cup sugar
1 tablespoon lemon juice
¾ cup ground almonds
2 large egg whites

Mix the pastry (see basic method, page 62), adding the lemon rind, sugar and salt at the final stage. Set aside for 1 hour in a cool place. Roll out on a floured board and use to line a 20-cm/8-inch (US: 8-inch) flan dish. Prick the base with a fork and put in the refrigerator to chill.

Meanwhile, wash the cherries and remove the stalks. Put them with half the sugar and the lemon juice into a covered ovenproof dish and cook in a moderately hot oven (200°C, 400°F, Gas Mark 6) for 30 minutes. Uncover the dish and allow to cool.

Bake the pastry case blind in a moderately hot oven (200°C, 400°F, Gas Mark 6) for 25 minutes. Scatter the ground almonds over the base of the pastry. Spoon the cherry mixture on top. Whisk the egg whites until stiff. Quickly and gently fold in the remaining sugar, then pile the meringue on to the cherries. Bake in a cool oven (150°C, 300°F, Gas Mark 2) for about 1 hour, until the meringue has set and the peaks are golden.

Apricots in Wine

(illustrated on page 83)

Total: 4870 kilojoules/1080 calories
♥

METRIC/IMPERIAL
0.5 kg/1 lb best quality dried apricots
about 300 ml/½ pint sweet white wine

AMERICAN
1 lb best quality dried apricots
about 1¼ cups sweet white wine

Wash the apricots and pat dry. Pack loosely into jars and pour on enough wine to cover. Screw on the lids tightly and leave for a week before eating.
Serve at the end of a meal with coffee.

Cherry and Almond Meringue (see recipe above)

Flamri de Semoule

The flavour of the white wine is unusual in this pretty sweet, and the fresh redcurrant sauce is truly delicious. A dinner party or family dish.

Per portion: 785 kilojoules/185 calories
Serves 4 ♥

METRIC/IMPERIAL	AMERICAN
225 g/8 oz redcurrants	½ lb red currants
castor sugar to sweeten	sugar to sweeten
300 ml/½ pint water	1¼ cups water
150 ml/¼ pint white wine	⅔ cup white wine
3 tablespoons semolina	¼ cup semolina
40 g/1½ oz castor sugar	3 tablespoons sugar
2 egg whites	2 egg whites

Purée the redcurrants in the liquidiser then sieve them to remove the tops and tails. Add sugar to taste.

Place the water and wine in a saucepan, bring to the boil and pour in the semolina. Simmer gently, stirring frequently, for about 10 minutes. Draw off the heat and cool. Beat in the sugar. Whisk the egg whites until stiff, fold in and pour into a lightly oiled jelly or charlotte mould. Cover and leave in the refrigerator for several hours.

Dip the base of the mould into very hot water, then turn out the flamri on a serving plate. Pour over the redcurrant sauce, and serve with more sauce and a bowl of yogurt, if liked.

Note: Other soft fruits, such as raspberries, blackcurrants, strawberries, can be used for the sauce.

Lemon Sorbet

Per portion: 765 kilojoules/180 calories
Serves 4 ♥

METRIC/IMPERIAL	AMERICAN
3 lemons	3 lemons
175 g/6 oz castor sugar	¾ cup sugar
600 ml/1 pint water	2½ cups water
1 egg white	1 egg white

Pare the rinds of the lemons with a potato peeler and squeeze the juice. Bring the sugar and water gently to the boil, stirring until the sugar has completely dissolved. Now boil fast for 4 minutes. Add the lemon rinds, bring back to the boil and boil fast for a further 2 minutes. Put the pan in a bowl of cold water to cool the syrup. Add the lemon juice. Strain into a freezer proof polythene carton and freeze to the mushy stage. Stir thoroughly, turning sides to centre. Fold in the stiffly whisked egg white and return to the freezer. Keep covered in the freezer to retain the fresh flavour.

Sorbets make the perfect end to a rich meal, and really serve to liven up jaded palates.

Fresh Lime Sorbet

This is a beautiful colour, and unbelievably fresh and welcome.

Per portion: 765 kilojoules/180 calories
Serves 4 ♥

METRIC/IMPERIAL	AMERICAN
rind and juice of 3 limes	rind and juice of 3 limes
175 g/6 oz castor sugar	¾ cup sugar
600 ml/1 pint water	2½ cups water
1 egg white	1 egg white

Use a potato peeler to remove the rind from the limes, carefully avoiding any pith.

Dissolve the sugar in the water and bring to the boil. Boil for 3 minutes. Add the peeled rind and boil for a further 3 minutes, uncovered and fast. Cool, then add the lime juice. Strain into a freezer proof polythene carton and freeze to the mushy stage. Remove, turn sides to centre and mix well. Carefully fold in the stiffly whisked egg white. Refreeze until firm.

Serve with tuiles d'amandes (see page 77).

Blackcurrant Water Ice

Per portion: 1115 kilojoules/265 calories
Serves 4 ♥

METRIC/IMPERIAL	AMERICAN
450 ml/¾ pint water	2 cups water
225 g/8 oz sugar	1 cup sugar
0.5 kg/1 lb blackcurrants, cooked in 150 ml/¼ pint water	1 lb black currants, cooked in ⅔ cup water
juice of 1 lemon	juice of 1 lemon
2 egg whites	2 egg whites

Boil the water and sugar together for 6 minutes to make a syrup. Cool. Blend the blackcurrants in a liquidiser then press through a sieve.

Mix the cooled sugar syrup with the blackcurrant purée and lemon juice. Pour into a freezer proof polythene carton and freeze to the mushy stage. Remove and stir thoroughly, turning sides to centre. Fold in the stiffly whisked egg whites and freeze again, carefully covered. Scoop into a chilled glass bowl to serve.

Celestial Bananas

A Creole dish.

Per portion: 815 kilojoules/195 calories
Serves 6 ♥

METRIC/IMPERIAL	AMERICAN
6 bananas, halved lengthways	6 bananas, halved lengthways
100 g/4 oz soft brown sugar	½ cup light brown sugar
juice of 1 lemon	juice of 1 lemon
grated rind of 1 orange	grated rind of 1 orange
6 tablespoons rum	½ cup rum

Lightly oil a shallow ovenproof dish. Lay the bananas in the bottom and pour over the sauce, made by mixing together the remaining ingredients. Cover loosely with foil and bake in the centre of a moderately hot oven (200°C, 400°F, Gas Mark 6) for 25 minutes. Baste once or twice during cooking.

Apricot Soufflé

Per portion: 880 kilojoules/225 calories
Serves 4 ♥

METRIC/IMPERIAL	AMERICAN
100 g/4 oz castor sugar	½ cup sugar
225 g/8 oz dried apricots, soaked	½ lb dried apricots, soaked
twist of lemon peel	twist of lemon peel
4 egg whites	4 egg whites

Lightly oil a 1-litre/2-pint (US: 2½-pint) soufflé dish and dust with castor sugar. Cook the apricots in the water in which they were soaked, with the lemon peel, for 30 minutes, until tender. Drain and remove the peel. Purée the apricots in a liquidiser, or press through a sieve. Stir in sugar to taste.

Whisk the egg whites until firm, fold gently and quickly into the apricot purée. Pour into the soufflé dish and cook in a moderately hot oven (200°C, 400°F, Gas Mark 6) for about 18 minutes. The soufflé should be firm sponge around the edge and creamy in the centre.

Honey Apples

Per portion: 625 kilojoules/150 calories
Serves 4 ♥

METRIC/IMPERIAL	AMERICAN
4 medium cooking apples, cored	4 medium baking apples, cored
1 tablespoon chopped nuts, toasted	1 tablespoon chopped nuts, toasted
1 tablespoon chopped dates	1 tablespoon chopped dates
juice of ½ lemon	juice of ½ lemon
2 tablespoons clear honey	2 tablespoons clear honey
½ teaspoon ground cinnamon	½ teaspoon ground cinnamon

Wash the apples and peel the top half. Place in an ovenproof dish. Mix the remaining ingredients together and use to fill the centre of the apples. Pour a little more honey over the apples and cook, covered, in a moderately hot oven (190°C, 375°F, Gas Mark 5) for about 45 minutes.

Cakes and Biscuits

What better on a cold winter's day than tea and cinnamon toast by the fire, with homemade fruit cake to follow? And for more summery occasions, try some of these home-baked biscuits to accompany fruit desserts, fools and sorbets.

Fruit Cake (see recipe page 76)
Hazelnut Biscuits (see recipe page 76)
Cinnamon Toast (see recipe page 76)

Fruit Cake

(illustrated on pages 74–75)

Total: 19870 kilojoules/4750 calories ♥

METRIC/IMPERIAL	AMERICAN
175 g/6 oz polyunsaturated margarine	¾ cup polyunsaturated margarine
225 g/8 oz soft brown sugar	1 cup light brown sugar
450 g/1 lb plain flour	4 cups all-purpose flour
½ teaspoon ground cinnamon	½ teaspoon ground cinnamon
350 g/12 oz mixed dried fruit	2 cups mixed dried fruit
3 tablespoons vinegar	¼ cup vinegar
175 ml/6 fl oz skimmed milk, at room temperature	¾ cup skimmed milk, at room temperature
1 heaped teaspoon bicarbonate of soda	1 heaped teaspoon baking soda

Line an 18-cm/7-inch (US: 7-inch) square cake tin with oiled and floured greaseproof paper.

Cream together the margarine and sugar until light. Sift the flour and cinnamon over the dried fruit in a bowl. Mix the creamed margarine and sugar with the flour and fruit. Work together thoroughly.

Put the vinegar in a large bowl and add the milk. Stir in the bicarbonate of soda, watching carefully as it will froth up. Stir at once into the fruit mixture and turn into the prepared tin. Bake in a moderately hot oven (190°C, 375°F, Gas Mark 5) for 30 minutes. Lay a piece of greaseproof paper over the top of the cake. Reduce the heat to 160°C, 325°F, Gas Mark 3 and bake for a further 1½ hours.

Hazelnut Biscuits

(illustrated on pages 74–75)

Each: 470 kilojoules/110 calories
Makes about 30 ♥

METRIC/IMPERIAL	AMERICAN
175 g/6 oz hazelnuts, ground	generous cup hazelnuts, ground
175 g/6 oz plain flour	1½ cups all-purpose flour
75 g/3 oz castor sugar	6 tablespoons sugar
175 g/6 oz polyunsaturated margarine	¾ cup polyunsaturated margarine
whole hazelnuts to decorate	whole hazelnuts to decorate

Mix all the ingredients together and knead to a dough. Put to one side in a cool place to stiffen.

Divide the dough into small equal-sized pieces and roll into balls. Press on to greased baking trays, flattening out, and place a whole hazelnut firmly on each biscuit. Bake in a moderately hot oven (190°C, 375°F, Gas Mark 5) for 10–12 minutes. Allow to cool slightly on the baking trays before transferring to a wire cooling rack.

Cinnamon Toast

(illustrated on pages 74–75)

Really good news, as P. G. Wodehouse would have said, for a winter's afternoon.

Per portion: 860 kilojoules/205 calories
Serves 6 ♥

METRIC/IMPERIAL	AMERICAN
6 slices white bread	6 slices white bread
polyunsaturated margarine to spread	polyunsaturated margarine to spread
3 tablespoons brown sugar	¼ cup brown sugar
2 teaspoons ground cinnamon	2 teaspoons ground cinnamon

Toast the bread on both sides and spread with margarine while still hot. Mix together the sugar and cinnamon and sprinkle on to the hot toast. Place under the grill until the sugar bubbles. Cut into fingers and serve immediately.

Tuiles d'Amandes

Very good, delicate and crisp. A lovely accompaniment to fruit desserts, such as fools and sorbets.

Each: 255 kilojoules/70 calories
Makes about 18 ♥

METRIC/IMPERIAL	AMERICAN
2 egg whites	2 egg whites
90 g/3½ oz castor sugar, sifted	7 tablespoons sugar, sifted
50 g/2 oz plain flour, sifted	½ cup all-purpose flour, sifted
¼ teaspoon vanilla essence	¼ teaspoon vanilla extract
¼ teaspoon almond essence	¼ teaspoon almond extract
25 g/1 oz almonds, shredded	¼ cup shredded almonds
50 g/2 oz polyunsaturated margarine, melted but not hot	¼ cup polyunsaturated margarine, melted but not hot

Whisk together the egg whites and castor sugar until thick. Fold in the sifted flour. Add the vanilla and almond essences, shredded almonds and margarine and mix all carefully together.

Line 2 large baking trays with non-stick baking paper and put small spoonfuls of the mixture on each, spaced well apart (the biscuits will spread out while cooking).

Bake in a moderately hot oven (190°C, 375°F, Gas Mark 5) for about 6 minutes, until pale gold. Remove from the oven, lift off the tuiles while still warm and curl quickly around the back of a rolling pin. Cool on a wire tray and store carefully in an airtight tin.

Baby Meringues

Each: 125 kilojoules/30 calories
Makes about 24 ♥

METRIC/IMPERIAL	AMERICAN
3 egg whites	3 egg whites
175 g/6 oz castor sugar	¾ cup sugar

Whisk the egg whites until really stiff. Add 2 tablespoons (US: 3 tablespoons) of the castor sugar and whisk again until stiff. Fold in the remaining sugar.

Line a large baking tray with non-stick baking paper. Using a star nozzle, pipe the meringue on to the paper in small star shapes. Bake in the coolest oven (110°C, 225°F, Gas Mark ¼) for about 4 hours, until the meringues can be easily removed from the paper with a palette knife.

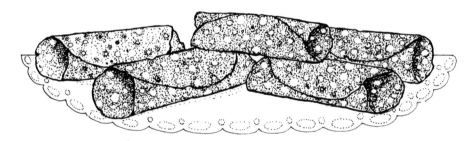

Brandy Snaps

(illustrated on pages 66–67)

Each: 255 kilojoules/70 calories
Makes about 30 ♥

METRIC/IMPERIAL	AMERICAN
100 g/4 oz golden syrup	⅓ cup corn syrup
100 g/4 oz brown sugar	½ cup light brown sugar
100 g/4 oz polyunsaturated margarine	½ cup polyunsaturated margarine
2 teaspoons lemon juice	2 teaspoons lemon juice
100 g/4 oz plain flour	1 cup all-purpose flour
¼ teaspoon salt	¼ teaspoon salt
1 teaspoon ground ginger	1 teaspoon ground ginger

Put the syrup, sugar and margarine in a saucepan and heat, stirring, until the sugar has melted. Cool slightly and stir in the lemon juice. Sift together the flour, salt and ginger and fold into the syrup mixture.

Place small spoonfuls, well apart, on to baking trays lined with non-stick paper. Cook for 8 minutes in a moderate oven (160°C, 325°F, Gas Mark 3). Allow to cool for a minute, then lift with a palette knife and shape the brandy snaps around the handle of a wooden spoon. Cool on a wire tray and store in an airtight tin.

Special Occasions

Special occasion menus do need careful planning, if the meal is to be the success it deserves. Christmas, Hallowe'en and New Year are all times when it is fun to be with friends and family, and when food is often the centre of the festivities. So try for two things – the most possible fun and good food with the least possible strain on the cook. These menus make good use of seasonal produce and help you to plan ahead, so after that sit back and enjoy yourself, and these very special times of year.

Hallowe'en Chicken with Sauce Diable (see recipe page 81)
Hot Glühwein (see recipe page 80)
Italian Leek and Pumpkin Soup (see recipe page 80)

Halloween

Hot Glühwein
Italian Leek and Pumpkin Soup
Hallowe'en Chicken with Sauce Diable
Oranges with Liqueur and Praline

Hot Glühwein

(illustrated on pages 78–79)

Per glass: 390 kilojoules/90 calories
Makes 8 glasses ♥

METRIC/IMPERIAL	AMERICAN
1 bottle red wine	1 bottle red wine
150 ml/¼ pint lemon squash	⅔ cup undiluted lemon drink
150 ml/¼ pint water	⅔ cup water
1 tablespoon rum	1 tablespoon rum
2 teaspoons sugar	2 teaspoons sugar
½ teaspoon ground ginger	½ teaspoon ground ginger
1 cinnamon stick, broken into pieces	1 cinnamon stick, broken into pieces
8 cloves	8 cloves

Mix all together and warm through gently until very hot but not boiling. Remove the cloves before serving.

Italian Leek and Pumpkin Soup

(illustrated on pages 78–79)

The hollowed-out shell of the pumpkin can be used as a tureen for this soup.

Per portion: 700 kilojoules/165 calories
Serves 8 ♥

METRIC/IMPERIAL	AMERICAN
1 Spanish onion, chopped	1 Spanish onion, chopped
50 g/2 oz chopped leek	½ cup chopped leek
2 tablespoons polyunsaturated oil	3 tablespoons polyunsaturated oil
0.5 kg/1 lb pumpkin flesh	1 lb pumpkin flesh
225 g/8 oz potatoes	½ lb potatoes
salt and freshly ground black pepper	salt and freshly ground black pepper
600 ml/1 pint skimmed milk	2½ cups skimmed milk
600 ml/1 pint hot chicken stock	2½ cups hot chicken stock
100 g/4 oz cooked long-grain rice	scant ⅔ cup cooked long-grain rice
150 ml/¼ pint natural low fat yogurt	⅔ cup plain low fat yogurt
chopped parsley to garnish	chopped parsley to garnish

Soften the onion and leek in the oil without browning. Dice the pumpkin flesh and potatoes and add with the seasoning, milk and stock to the onions. Bring to the boil, cover and simmer for 45 minutes, stirring frequently.

Blend the soup in the liquidiser or press through a sieve. Return to the pan and add the cooked rice and most of the yogurt. Reheat gently before serving, topped with the remaining yogurt and sprinkled with parsley.

Hallowe'en Chicken with Sauce Diable

(illustrated on pages 78–79)

Per portion: 1525 kilojoules/365 calories
Serves 8 ♥

METRIC/IMPERIAL	AMERICAN
8 chicken portions, skinned	8 chicken portions, skinned
150 ml/¼ pint polyunsaturated oil	⅔ cup polyunsaturated oil
sea salt and freshly ground black pepper	sea salt and freshly ground black pepper
6 tablespoons Dijon mustard	½ cup Dijon mustard
75 g/3 oz fresh white breadcrumbs, dried in the oven	1½ cups fresh soft white bread crumbs, dried in the oven
For the Sauce Diable	*For the Sauce Diable*
4 shallots, finely chopped	4 shallots, finely chopped
2 tablespoons black peppercorns, crushed	3 tablespoons black peppercorns, crushed
150 ml/¼ pint dry white wine	⅔ cup dry white wine
3 tablespoons wine vinegar	¼ cup wine vinegar
150 ml/¼ pint light stock	⅔ cup light stock
2 tablespoons chopped herbs (tarragon, chervil and parsley)	3 tablespoons chopped herbs (tarragon, chervil, and parsley)
2 tablespoons snipped chives	3 tablespoons snipped chives
Garnish	*Garnish*
8 lemon wedges	8 lemon wedges
1 bunch watercress	1 bunch watercress

Brush the chicken portions all over with oil. Season with salt and pepper. Cook in a pan under a moderately hot grill for 15 minutes, turning after 8 minutes. Remove the chicken from the grill and coat each portion with mustard. Dip in the breadcrumbs, covering well. Replace the chicken under the grill and sprinkle a little more oil on the breadcrumbs as they start to brown. Cook until the chicken and breadcrumbs are golden brown, turning. The total cooking time should be about 35 minutes, depending on the heat of your grill.

To make the sauce, boil the shallots, peppercorns, wine and vinegar for about 5 minutes, to reduce to about half its original volume. Add the stock and boil for a further 4 minutes. Add the herbs, reheat, and pour into a hot sauceboat.

Place the chicken portions in a serving basket. Arrange the lemon wedges and watercress over the chicken. Hand the sauce separately and serve with baked jacket potatoes.

Oranges with Liqueur and Praline

Per portion: 1350 kilojoules/325 calories
Serves 8 ♥

METRIC/IMPERIAL	AMERICAN
8 large oranges	8 large oranges
150 ml/¼ pint orange liqueur	⅔ cup orange liqueur
150 g/5 oz granulated sugar	⅔ cup sugar
175 g/6 oz hazelnuts, chopped	1 cup chopped hazelnuts

Peel the oranges entirely free of pith with a sharp knife. Slice and arrange in a glass serving dish. Sprinkle over the liqueur.

Dissolve the sugar very slowly in a frying pan and leave until it is a brown syrup. (Don't stir, just keep your nerve). Add the chopped hazelnuts and stir for two minutes. Pour into a well-oiled roasting tin and leave to set. When set hard, remove the praline from the tin, wrap in a clean cloth and break up with a hammer. Sprinkle over the marinated oranges.

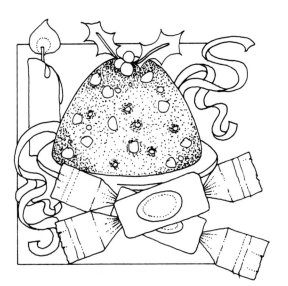

Christmas

Traditional Roast Turkey
Cranberry Sauce (see page 61)
Rich and Light Christmas Pudding
Brandy Butter (see page 65)
Lemon Mincemeat
Apricots in Wine (see page 70)

Traditional Roast Turkey

Per average portion with stuffing:
1450 kilojoules/370 calories

♥

<table>
<tr><th>METRIC/IMPERIAL</th><th>AMERICAN</th></tr>
<tr><td>1 (4.5-kg/10-lb) turkey</td><td>1 (10-lb) turkey</td></tr>
<tr><td>polyunsaturated margarine, melted</td><td>polyunsaturated margarine, melted</td></tr>
<tr><td>1 tablespoon dried basil</td><td>1 tablespoon dried basil</td></tr>
<tr><td>salt and freshly ground black pepper</td><td>salt and freshly ground black pepper</td></tr>
<tr><td>600 ml/1 pint good stock</td><td>2½ cups good stock</td></tr>
<tr><td>5 tablespoons port</td><td>6 tablespoons port</td></tr>
<tr><td>1 tablespoon cornflour</td><td>1 tablespoon cornstarch</td></tr>
<tr><td>For the stuffings</td><td>For the stuffings</td></tr>
<tr><td>0.5 kg/1 lb chestnuts</td><td>1 lb chestnuts</td></tr>
<tr><td>175 g/6 oz mashed potato</td><td>¾ cup mashed potato</td></tr>
<tr><td>salt and freshly ground black pepper</td><td>salt and freshly ground black pepper</td></tr>
<tr><td>65 g/2½ oz fresh breadcrumbs, fried until golden in polyunsaturated oil and margarine</td><td>1¼ cups fresh soft bread crumbs, fried until golden in polyunsaturated oil and margarine</td></tr>
<tr><td>1 heaped tablespoon sultanas</td><td>1 heaped tablespoon seedless white raisins</td></tr>
<tr><td>1 clove garlic, crushed</td><td>1 clove garlic, crushed</td></tr>
<tr><td>2 sticks celery, finely chopped</td><td>2 stalks celery, finely chopped</td></tr>
<tr><td>2 tablespoons chopped parsley</td><td>3 tablespoons chopped parsley</td></tr>
<tr><td>grated rind of 1 lemon</td><td>grated rind of 1 lemon</td></tr>
<tr><td>little grated fresh root ginger</td><td>little grated fresh ginger root</td></tr>
<tr><td>3 tablespoons medium dry sherry</td><td>¼ cup medium dry sherry</td></tr>
</table>

Prepare the stuffings for the neck and carcass in advance. Make a slit on the rounded side of the chestnuts. Drop, four at a time, into small pans of boiling water for 3 minutes. Peel and skin. Cook the peeled chestnuts gently in fresh boiling water for about 20 minutes. Mash with a fork. Mix a quarter of the chestnuts with the mashed potato, seasoning and a little melted margarine. Use to stuff the neck of the bird. Mix the remaining chestnuts with the rest of the stuffing ingredients and use to stuff the turkey carcass.

Stand the bird in a large roasting tin. Brush all over with melted margarine and sprinkle with basil and seasoning. Pour the stock around the bird and cover the tin loosely with a piece of greased foil. Cook in a moderate oven (180°C, 350°F, Gas Mark 4), allowing 15–20 minutes per 0.5 kg/1 lb (US: 1 lb), plus 20 minutes extra. Turn the turkey, on its side or upright, every 30 minutes and baste with the pan juices.

Remove the foil 20 minutes before the end of the cooking time, to brown the bird, turning it breast sides up. Pour off the pan juices to make gravy. Skim off all the fat and boil up the juices with the port. Moisten the cornflour with a little cold water and stir into the gravy, to thicken. Keep warm in a sauceboat until ready to serve.

82

Rich and Light Christmas Pudding (see recipe page 84)
Apricots in Wine (see recipe page 70)
Lemon Mincemeat (see recipe page 84)

Rich and Light Christmas Pudding

(illustrated on page 83)

Per portion: 2060 kilojoules/500 calories
Makes 3 puddings each to serve 8 ♥

METRIC/IMPERIAL	AMERICAN
450 g/1 lb currants	3 cups currants
450 g/1 lb sultanas	3 cups seedless white raisins
450 g/1 lb raisins	3 cups raisins
100 g/4 oz chopped mixed peel	⅔ cup chopped candied peel
450 g/1 lb polyunsaturated margarine	2 cups polyunsaturated margarine
450 g/1 lb dark soft brown sugar	2 cups dark brown sugar
175 g/6 oz self-raising flour, sifted	1½ cups all-purpose flour, sifted with 1½ teaspoons baking powder
1 rounded teaspoon mixed spice	1 rounded teaspoon mixed spice
1 rounded teaspoon grated nutmeg	1 rounded teaspoon grated nutmeg
450 g/1 lb fresh brown breadcrumbs	8 cups fresh soft brown bread crumbs
rind and juice of 1 lemon	rind and juice of 1 lemon
5 eggs	5 eggs
150 ml/¼ pint rum or brandy	⅔ cup rum or brandy
4 tablespoons black treacle	⅓ cup molasses
300 ml/½ pint Guinness	1¼ cups dark beer or stout

Well oil three 1-litre/2-pint (US: 2½-pint) pudding basins and put a disc of oiled greaseproof paper in the base of each, to help the puddings turn out easily when served.

Wash and dry the fruit. Place in a large bowl with the chopped peel. Cream the margarine and sugar together until light and fluffy and mix into the dried fruits. Stir in the flour, mixed spice, nutmeg and breadcrumbs. Add the grated lemon rind and strained juice. In a smaller bowl, beat together the eggs, rum or brandy and treacle. Add the Guinness and then gradually combine with the fruit mixture.

Divide this mixture between the basins and cover each with greased greaseproof paper or foil (making a centre fold to allow for expansion). Tuck over the outside rim and secure with string. Allow to stand in a cool place overnight.

Steam the puddings individually in the top of a double boiler, for at least 6 hours. Cover with fresh tops and store in a cool place.

When required to serve, steam for 2–3 hours. Turn out and top with a sprig of holly. Prick with a fork. Flame with warm brandy or rum and serve with plenty of brandy butter.

Ideally, make the puddings well in advance of Christmas, and store for a few weeks to allow the flavours to mature.

Lemon Mincemeat

(illustrated on page 83)

Total: 4000 kilojoules/3480 calories
Makes about 1.75 kg/4 lb (US: 4 lb) ♥

METRIC/IMPERIAL	AMERICAN
rind and juice of 3 lemons	rind and juice of 3 lemons
225 g/8 oz dark soft brown sugar	1 cup dark brown sugar
0.5 kg/1 lb cooking apples, peeled and cored	1 lb baking apples, peeled and cored
225 g/8 oz currants	1½ cups currants
225 g/8 oz seedless raisins	1½ cups seeded raisins
100 g/4 oz polyunsaturated margarine	½ cup polyunsaturated margarine
½ teaspoon salt	½ teaspoon salt
1 teaspoon ground cloves	1 teaspoon ground cloves
1 teaspoon ground nutmeg	1 teaspoon ground nutmeg
1 teaspoon ground ginger	1 teaspoon ground ginger
150 ml/¼ pint brandy or sherry	⅔ cup brandy or sherry

Pare the rinds from the lemons with a potato peeler and simmer gently in a little boiling water until soft and tender, about 5 minutes. Drain.

Chop the rinds finely into a large bowl and mix with the sugar. Grate the apples and add with the currants, raisins, margarine, salt and spices. Mix well together and add the brandy and lemon juice. Stir thoroughly and pack into clean, dry jars. Cover with waxed jam pot circles and transparent covers.

New Year

Winter Vegetable Soup (see page 20)
Faisan en Casserole
Grapes with Kirsch and Lemon Sorbet

Faisan en Casserole

Per average portion:
3125 kilojoules/750 calories
Serves 6 ♥

METRIC/IMPERIAL	AMERICAN
a brace of pheasant	a brace of pheasant
2 tablespoons polyunsaturated oil	3 tablespoons polyunsaturated oil
2 onions, chopped	2 onions, chopped
2 tablespoons flour	3 tablespoons all-purpose flour
600 ml/1 pint good stock	2½ cups good stock
2 teaspoons redcurrant jelly	2 teaspoons red currant jelly
rind and juice of 1 orange	rind and juice of 1 orange
150 ml/¼ pint port or red wine	⅔ cup port or red wine
bouquet garni	bouquet garni
salt and freshly ground black pepper	salt and freshly ground black pepper
4 slices bread, crusts removed	4 slices bread, crusts removed
oil to fry	oil to fry
chopped parsley to garnish	chopped parsley to garnish

Brown the pheasants gently in a casserole with the oil, turning and making sure they don't catch. Transfer to a plate and keep warm.

Fry the onions gently in the remaining fat until softened. Sprinkle over the flour and stir until blended. Gradually add the stock, stirring, then the redcurrant jelly, grated orange rind and juice, red wine, bouquet garni and seasoning. Simmer, stirring, for 1 minute. Return the pheasants to the pan and spoon the sauce over them.

Cover and cook slowly on top of the cooker, or in a moderate oven (160°C, 325°F, Gas Mark 3) for 1 hour, until the meat is tender. Remove the pheasants and carve and joint them; cover and keep warm.

Cut the bread slices with a small heart-shaped cutter, fry in oil and drain on kitchen paper. Keep warm. When ready to serve, arrange the pheasant pieces on a large heated serving dish, spoon a little sauce over and dredge parsley down the centre. Surround with the heart-shaped croûtons. Heat through the rest of the sauce and hand separately.

Grapes with Kirsch and Lemon Sorbet

Per portion: 1000 kilojoules/235 calories
Serves 6 ♥

METRIC/IMPERIAL	AMERICAN
225 g/8 oz each black and green grapes, halved and pipped	½ lb each purple and white grapes, halved and pipped
3 tablespoons castor sugar	¼ cup sugar
3 tablespoons Kirsch	¼ cup Kirsch
600 ml/1 pint lemon sorbet (see page 72)	2½ cups lemon sorbet (see page 72)
mint sprigs to garnish	mint sprigs to garnish

Put green grapes into one bowl and black into another. Spoon castor sugar and Kirsch, mixed together, over the grapes. Chill in the refrigerator.

When it is time to serve, layer grapes and sorbet in individual glasses and garnish each with a mint sprig.

Buffet Parties

A buffet party can be the ideal way to entertain—a gathering of friends, good food and wine and a relaxed and happy hostess guarantee the success of the occasion. The recipes here are mostly to serve eight people; increase the quantities as necessary, and for starters and desserts take your pick from the recipes in those sections. Remember that buffet party fare should ideally be fork, spoon or finger food—unless you have enough chairs to seat a crowd!

Andalusian Chicken (see recipe page 88)

Andalusian Chicken

(illustrated on pages 86–87)

Per portion: 2000 kilojoules/480 calories
Serves 8 ♥

METRIC/IMPERIAL
1 (2-kg/4½-lb) roasting chicken
polyunsaturated oil
salt and freshly ground black pepper
1 teaspoon dried mixed herbs
225 g/8 oz Spanish onions, chopped
0.5 kg/1 lb green peppers, deseeded and diced
4 tomatoes, peeled, deseeded and roughly chopped
1 chorizo sausage, sliced (optional)
2 cloves garlic, crushed
4 tablespoons polyunsaturated oil
225 g/8 oz peas, cooked
350 g/12 oz long-grain rice
pinch saffron powder
1 bay leaf
Garnish
2 whole prawns
lemon slice
chopped parsley

AMERICAN
1 (4½-lb) roasting chicken
polyunsaturated oil
salt and freshly ground black pepper
1 teaspoon dried mixed herbs
½ lb Spanish onions, chopped
1 lb green peppers, deseeded and diced
4 tomatoes, peeled, deseeded and roughly chopped
1 chorizo sausage, sliced (optional)
2 cloves garlic, crushed
⅓ cup polyunsaturated oil
½ lb peas, cooked
1½ cups long-grain rice
pinch saffron powder
1 bay leaf
Garnish
2 whole shrimp
lemon slice
chopped parsley

Rub the chicken with oil, sprinkle with salt, pepper and herbs and stand in a roasting tin. Pour a cup of water around the chicken. Cover loosely with greased greaseproof paper or foil and roast in a moderately hot oven (200°C, 400°F, Gas Mark 6) for 1½ hours. Cool the chicken slightly, then strip the flesh from the bones, cut into bite-sized pieces and set aside. Use the carcass and giblets to make chicken stock in which to cook the rice.

Fry the onions, peppers, tomatoes, sausage and garlic gently in the oil until soft and golden. Stir in the cooked drained peas.

Cook the rice in 900 ml/1½ pints (US: 3¾ cups) chicken stock, with the saffron and bay leaf, for about 10 minutes, until tender. Drain if necessary (the rice should be quite dry) and remove the bay leaf.

Now fold the chicken and rice into the onion mixture. Pile into a large, heated serving dish and garnish with the prawns and lemon slice. Serve sprinkled with parsley.

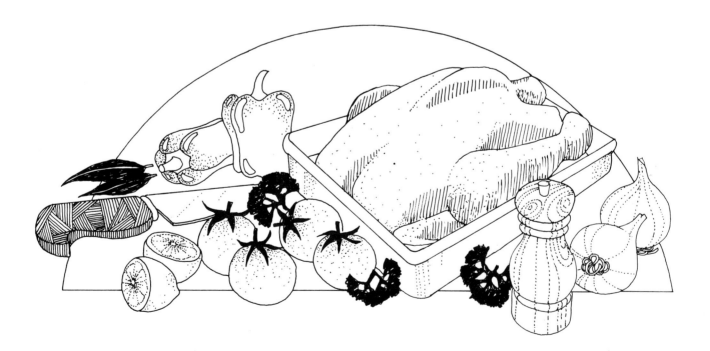

Cold Salmon

For a very special occasion this, such as a small wedding reception or silver wedding anniversary party.

Per 100 g/4 oz (US: ¼ lb) portion: 670 kilojoules/180 calories ♥

METRIC/IMPERIAL	AMERICAN
1 salmon or salmon trout (not more than 4.5 kg/10 lb in weight)	1 salmon or salmon trout (not more than 10 lb in weight)
For the court bouillon	*For the court bouillon*
enough water to cover the fish	enough water to cover the fish
1 onion, sliced	1 onion, sliced
½ lemon, sliced	½ lemon, sliced
bouquet garni	bouquet garni
1 carrot, sliced	1 carrot, sliced
12 black peppercorns	12 black peppercorns
Garnish	*Garnish*
½ cucumber, thinly sliced	½ cucumber, thinly sliced
18 whole prawns	18 whole shrimp
lettuce hearts	lettuce hearts
1 bunch watercress	1 bunch watercress
mint leaves	mint leaves
6 tiny salmon pink roses, if available	6 tiny salmon pink roses, if available
2 lemons, sliced	2 lemons, sliced

Simmer together the ingredients for the court bouillon for 30 minutes. Allow to cool.

Make sure that the inside of the fish is perfectly cleaned, or the tailpiece will taste bitter. Place the fish in a fish kettle in the *cold* prepared court bouillon and cover. Bring very slowly to the boil. Boil for exactly 3 minutes. Remove from the heat and put the kettle in a cold place for at least 12 hours. However large your salmon this method will work, because a larger fish will take longer to cool down.

Lift out the fish on its drainer and slide gently on to a large dish. (I once used a plank of wood, cut to size and covered with foil, as a serving dish). Skin the salmon carefully. Turn it over and skin the other side. Lay slices of cucumber down the entire centre length of the salmon. Peel the prawns, except for their heads (this looks prettier and leaves something firm to pick them up by) and lay on the cucumber slices. Tuck tiny lettuce hearts around the salmon and place a bunch of watercress where the head should be.

Put mint leaves and small salmon pink roses at each end of this really impressive dish – but do resist tomatoes, radishes or anything which might be a colour clash. Add fine curls of sliced lemon to your arrangement – but beware of gilding the lily!

Accompany the salmon with cucumber sauce (see page 65) and mayonnaise (see page 60).

Lamb Korma

(illustrated opposite)

A gift of a small collection of curry spices gave me the push I needed to start experimenting with Indian cookery. Once you have tried it, the tin of blended curry powder goes to the back of the shelf! This dish is mild and scented.

Per portion: 3125 kilojoules/700 calories
Serves 8 ♥ ♥ ♥

METRIC/IMPERIAL	AMERICAN
1.5 kg/3 lb boneless lamb, shoulder or leg	3 lb boneless lamb, shoulder or leg
300 ml/½ pint natural low fat yogurt	1¼ cups plain low fat yogurt
½ teaspoon crushed cardamom	½ teaspoon crushed cardamom
1 teaspoon ground cumin	1 teaspoon ground cumin
1½ teaspoons ground turmeric	1½ teaspoons ground turmeric
100 g/4 oz grated coconut	1⅓ cups grated coconut
6 tablespoons polyunsaturated oil	½ cup polyunsaturated oil
3 Spanish onions, chopped	3 Spanish onions, chopped
2 cloves garlic, crushed	2 cloves garlic, crushed
1 teaspoon ground ginger	1 teaspoon ground ginger
salt and freshly ground black pepper	salt and freshly ground black pepper
½ teaspoon cayenne pepper	½ teaspoon cayenne pepper
1 cinnamon stick	1 cinnamon stick
6 cloves	6 cloves
3 tomatoes, peeled and quartered	3 tomatoes, peeled and quartered
juice of ½ lemon	juice of ½ lemon

Trim the meat of any excess fat and cut into 2.5-cm/1-inch (US: 1-inch) cubes. Mix the yogurt with the cardamom, cumin and turmeric. Add the lamb and turn the pieces of meat until well coated. Cover and leave in a cool place for 1 hour.

Simmer the coconut in 300 ml/½ pint (US: 1¼ cups) water for 15 minutes. Strain the coconut and keep the liquor.

Heat the oil in a large pan and fry the onions and garlic until soft and golden. Add the cubes of lamb and yogurt and cook, stirring, for about 5 minutes. Mix in the ginger, black pepper, cayenne, cinnamon stick and cloves. Add the tomatoes and salt to taste, then stir in the coconut milk. Bring gently back to the boil, cover and simmer for about 1 hour. Remove the lid if the sauce needs to reduce a little. At the end of the cooking time remove the cinnamon stick and cloves. Finally adjust the seasoning, add the lemon juice and turn into a hot dish. Serve with rice and the usual side dishes that go with curry; tomato and onion, chutney, poppadoms, etc.

Chicken, Celery and Walnut Salad

Per portion: 2240 kilojoules/535 calories
Serves 8 ♥

METRIC/IMPERIAL	AMERICAN
1 (2-kg/4½-lb) chicken, with giblets	1 (4½-lb) chicken, with giblets
2 tablespoons polyunsaturated oil	3 tablespoons polyunsaturated oil
3 tarragon sprigs	3 tarragon sprigs
300 ml/½ pint water	1¼ cups water
1 large head celery, chopped	1 large bunch celery, chopped
100 g/4 oz walnuts, coarsely chopped	1 cup coarsely chopped walnuts
2 tablespoons chopped parsley	3 tablespoons chopped parsley
300 ml/½ pint French dressing (see page 60)	1¼ cups French dressing (see page 60)
salt and freshly ground black pepper	salt and freshly ground black pepper
Garnish	*Garnish*
watercress	watercress
lettuce hearts	lettuce hearts

Remove the giblets and brush the chicken with oil. Sprinkle with the chopped tarragon leaves and place in a roasting tin. Surround with the giblets and pour in the water. Cover the tin loosely with greaseproof paper or foil and cook in a moderately hot oven (200°C, 400°F, Gas Mark 6) for 1–1¼ hours. Allow to cool.

Remove all the chicken meat from the bone and cut into bite-sized pieces. Combine with the celery, walnuts and parsley. Toss in enough French dressing to moisten, and season to taste.

Pile on to a serving dish and surround with small bunches of watercress and lettuce hearts.

Lamb Korma (see recipe above)

Ham in Parsley Jelly

Per portion: 1150 kilojoules/275 calories
Serves 8 ♥ ♥

METRIC/IMPERIAL	AMERICAN
1 shin or knuckle of veal, sawn into pieces	1 shin bone of veal, sawn into pieces
2 calf's feet, coarsely chopped	2 calf's feet, coarsely chopped
bouquet garni	bouquet garni
4 small onions	4 small onions
8 black peppercorns	8 black peppercorns
600 ml/1 pint dry cider	2½ cups dry cider
1 (1.25-kg/2½-lb) piece ham (all fat trimmed off)	1 (2½-lb) piece ham (all fat trimmed off)
polyunsaturated oil	polyunsaturated oil
3 tablespoons finely chopped parsley	¼ cup finely chopped parsley
1 tablespoon wine vinegar	1 tablespoon wine vinegar
4 tablespoons dry white wine or cider	⅓ cup dry white wine or cider

Put the first six ingredients into a large pan and bring to the boil, adding enough water to cover the bones. Remove the scum as it rises to the surface. Cover the pan and cook gently for 3 hours, to make a strong stock. Trim the ham of all fat and soak in cold water for the same time, to remove some of the saltiness. Drain and place in the strained veal stock. Bring back to the boil and remove the scum. Cover and simmer until the ham is tender, about 2 hours. This simmering must be very slow, or the ham will toughen. Cool in the stock.

Lightly oil a 1.75-litre/3-pint (US: 4-pint) glass bowl and sprinkle with a little parsley. Dice the ham coarsely and press gently into the prepared dish. Strain the stock into a clean bowl through a fine sieve; cool. Skim all the fat from the surface, and moisten the ham with a very little stock. Restrain the remaining stock through a sieve lined with a wet flannel cloth. Cool until syrupy. Stir in the vinegar, the remaining parsley and white wine or cider. Pour this over the ham chunks and put it in the refrigerator to set. Serve in slices from the dish or turn out on a serving plate.

Salmon Mousse

Per portion: 855 kilojoules/215 calories
Serves 8 ♥

METRIC/IMPERIAL	AMERICAN
450 g/1 lb cold cooked salmon, flaked	1 lb cold cooked salmon, flaked
50 g/2 oz polyunsaturated margarine	¼ cup polyunsaturated margarine
50 g/2 oz flour	½ cup all-purpose flour
300 ml/½ pint skimmed milk	1¼ cups skimmed milk
salt and white pepper	salt and white pepper
tarragon sprig or bay leaf	tarragon sprig or bay leaf
15 g/½ oz gelatine	2 envelopes gelatin
2 tablespoons medium dry sherry	3 tablespoons medium dry sherry
3 egg whites, stiffly whisked	3 egg whites, stiffly beaten
Garnish	*Garnish*
lettuce hearts or watercress	lettuce hearts or watercress
½ cucumber, thinly sliced	½ cucumber, thinly sliced

Pound the salmon in a bowl with the end of a rolling pin. Make a béchamel sauce with the margarine, flour, milk, seasoning and tarragon (see page 61).

Soften the gelatine in the sherry then dissolve in a bowl over a saucepan of boiling water. Stir into the béchamel sauce and remove the tarragon sprig. Combine thoroughly with the salmon and fold in the stiffly whisked egg whites. Transfer to a lightly oiled 1.75-litre/3-pint (US: 4-pint) soufflé dish and chill in the refrigerator until set.

To turn out, dip the dish quickly in a bowl of boiling water and run a knife around the inside edge. Invert on to a serving dish, surround with lettuce hearts or watercress and garnish with cucumber slices.

As this is a fairly rich dish, the portions served should be modest. It makes an equally good starter for a special dinner party.

Lemon and Chicken Pie

(illustrated on the jacket)

Per portion: 4300 kilojoules/1010 calories
Serves 4 ♥

METRIC/IMPERIAL	AMERICAN
350 g/12 oz quantity shortcrust pastry (see page 62)	¾ lb quantity shortcrust pastry (see page 62)
4 young carrots, sliced	4 young carrots, sliced
1 (113-g/4-oz) packet frozen peas	1 (4-oz) packet frozen peas
50 g/2 oz polyunsaturated margarine	¼ cup polyunsaturated margarine
2 tablespoons flour	3 tablespoons all-purpose flour
300 ml/½ pint skimmed milk	1¼ cups skimmed milk
225 g/8 oz cooked chicken, chopped	1 cup chopped cooked chicken
grated rind of ½ lemon	grated rind of ½ lemon
1 tablespoon chopped parsley	1 tablespoon chopped parsley
salt and pepper	salt and pepper
parsley sprig to garnish	parsley sprig to garnish

First make the pastry. Cover and chill in the refrigerator while making the filling.

Cook the carrots and peas, drain and set aside. Melt the margarine and stir in the flour. Add the milk, half at a time, and stir over a low heat until it has been simmering for several minutes. Combine the carrots, peas, chicken, lemon rind and parsley all together. Mix into the sauce and season to taste.

Line the base of a greased and floured heart-shaped baking tin with half the pastry rolled out thin. Prick with a fork and damp the edges. Fill with the chicken mixture, roll out the remaining pastry and lay on top, pressing down the edges to seal. Trim the edges and knock up, brush with skimmed milk and bake in a moderately hot oven (190°C, 375°F, Gas Mark 5) for about 40 minutes. Garnish with a parsley sprig.

Angel Cake

This can be filled with strawberries, which have been sprinkled with castor sugar and a little lemon juice, or iced with a glacé icing – either white or chocolate.

Total: 2930 kilojoules/700 calories ♥

METRIC/IMPERIAL	AMERICAN
40 g/1½ oz plain white flour	6 tablespoons all-purpose flour
25 g/1 oz cornflour	¼ cup cornstarch
1 teaspoon baking powder	1 teaspoon baking powder
125 g/4½ oz castor sugar	generous ½ cup sugar
5 egg whites	5 egg whites
¼ teaspoon salt	¼ teaspoon salt
½ teaspoon cream of tartar	½ teaspoon cream of tartar
1 teaspoon vanilla essence	1 teaspoon vanilla extract

Sift the first three ingredients together several times to incorporate air and blend well. Sift the castor sugar with a tablespoon of the flour mixture.

Whisk the egg whites with the salt and cream of tartar until quite stiff. Fold in the dry ingredients very quickly and gently, and then the vanilla essence, sprinkled over.

Pour into a lightly oiled and floured ring tin. Cook in a moderately hot oven (190°C, 375°F, Gas Mark 5) for about 25 minutes, until the cake feels springy and shrinks slightly from the sides of the tin. Invert on a wire rack to cool. Turn out when cold.

Index

Almond:
  Cherry and almond meringue 70
  Trout with almonds 30
  Tuiles d'amandes 77
Andalusian chicken 88
Angel cake 93
Apple:
  Danish apple charlotte 69
  Honey apples 73
Apricot:
  Apricot soufflé 73
  Apricot yogurt 68
  Apricots in wine 70
Artichoke:
  Artichoke soup 21
  Topinambours provençale 53
Aubergine:
  Aubergine casserole 52
  Moussaka 40
Avocado pear:
  Avocado and caviar mousse 14
  Avocado pear salad 57

Banana:
  Celestial bananas 73
Batter for pancakes 62
Bean:
  French beans and mushrooms vinaigrette 54
Béchamel sauce 61
Beef:
  Casserole of beef with wine 41
  Moussaka 40
  Old English casserole of beef 40
  Roast beef fillet 41
  Spaghetti alla marinara 38
Biscuits:
  Baby meringues 77
  Brandy snaps 77
  Hazelnut biscuits 76
  Tuiles d'amandes 77
Blackcurrant water ice 73
Braised fennel 52
Brandy:
  Brandy butter 65
  Brandy snaps 77
  Peaches in brandy 69
Bream:
  Psari plaki 29
Buckling, smoked 12
Buffet parties 88–93

Cabbage:
  Coleslaw 56
  Obbie's salad 56
  Red cabbage 52

Cake:
  Angel cake 93
  Fruit cake 76
Carrot:
  Carrot and tomato soup 25
  Carrot salad 56
Casseroles:
  Aubergine casserole 52
  Casserole of beef with wine 41
  Civet de lièvre 48
  Faisan en casserole 85
  Italian veal casserole 38
  Old English casserole of beef 40
Celery:
  Chicken, celery and walnut salad 90
Celestial bananas 73
Cereals 7
Cheese, soft curd 64
Cherry:
  Cherry and almond meringue 70
Chicken:
  Andalusian chicken 88
  Chicken, celery and walnut salad 90
  Chicken en cocotte 44
  Chicken with white wine and tarragon 44
  Grilled devilled chicken 45
  Hallowe'en chicken with sauce diable 81
  Lemon and chicken pie 93
  Paprika chicken 49
  Roast chicken with tarragon 46
  Stuffed pot-roasted chicken 45
Cholesterol and diet 6–8
Christmas menu 82–4
Christmas pudding, rich and light 84
Cinnamon toast 76
Civet de lièvre 48
Cod:
  Fish pie 33
  Portuguese cod 28
Coleslaw 56
Compote of rhubarb 68
Cooking, ways of 7
Country vegetable soup 25
Courgette 53:
  Courgette and cucumber soup 22
  Courgettes provençale 53
Court bouillon 89
Cranberry sauce 61
Cucumber:
  Cucumber and courgette soup 22

Cucumber and mint sauce 64
  Cucumber sauce 65
  Iced cucumber soup 24
Cumberland sauce 60
Curd cheese, soft 64

Dairy produce 7
Danish apple charlotte 69
Desserts:
  Angel cake 93
  Apricot soufflé 73
  Apricot yogurt 68
  Apricots in wine 70
  Blackcurrant water ice 73
  Celestial bananas 73
  Cherry and almond meringue 70
  Compote of rhubarb 68
  Danish apple charlotte 69
  Flamri de semoule 72
  Fresh lime sorbet 72
  Fresh orange jelly 69
  Geranium creams 68
  Gooseberry fool with brandy snaps 68
  Grapes with Kirsch and lemon sorbet 85
  Honey apples 73
  Lemon sorbet 72
  Oranges with liqueur and praline 81
  Pancakes St Clements 70
  Peaches in brandy 69
  Rich and light Christmas pudding 84
Duckling with olives 46

Eels, smoked 12
Eggs 7

Faisan en casserole 85
Fennel:
  Braised fennel 52
Fish. See also Cod, Haddock etc.
  Fish in a brick 28
  Fish pie 33
  Garlic and tarragon sauce for steamed fish 29
  Psari plaki 29
  Smoked fish starters 12
Flamri de semoule 72
French beans and mushrooms vinaigrette 54
French dressing 60
French onion soup 20
Fruit. See also Apple, Apricot etc.
Fruit cake 76

Game see Poultry and game

Garlic and tarragon sauce for steamed fish 29
Gazpacho 22
Geranium creams 68
Glühwein, hot 80
Gooseberry fool with brandy snaps 68
Grapes with Kirsch and lemon sorbet 85
Gravad lax 16
Grilled devilled chicken 45

Haddock:
  Fish pie 33
  Kedgeree 32
Hallowe'en menu 80–1
Ham:
  Ham in parsley jelly 92
  Saltimbocca 37
Hare:
  Civet de lièvre 48
Hazelnut and leek quiche 17
Hazelnut biscuits 76
Honey apples 73
Horseradish sauce 40

Iced cucumber soup 24
Ices:
  Blackcurrant water ice 73
  Fresh lime sorbet 72
  Lemon sorbet 72
Italian leek and pumpkin soup 80
Italian veal casserole 38

Kedgeree 32

Lamb:
  Lamb korma 90
  Moussaka 40
  Navarin de mouton 37
  Roast lamb 36
Leek:
  Hazelnut and leek quiche 17
  Italian leek and pumpkin soup 80
  Vichyssoise 24
Lemon:
  Lemon and chicken pie 93
  Lemon mincemeat 84
  Lemon sorbet 72
  Mackerel with lemon and bay leaves 28

Lime:
  Fresh lime sorbet 72
Low cholesterol soured cream 65

Mackerel:
  Mackerel with lemon and bay leaves 28

Mackerel with yogurt and
    chives 29
Smoked mackerel 12
Margarine 7
Mayonnaise 60
Meat. *See also* Beef, Lamb etc.
    and Poultry
    Moussaka 40
    Types of meat to choose 7
Melon with Vermouth 13
Meringues, baby 77
Mincemeat, lemon 84
Moussaka 40
Mousse:
    Avocado and caviar mousse 14
    Salmon mousse 92
Mushroom:
    French beans and mushrooms
        vinaigrette 54
    Mushrooms en cocotte 12
    Plaice with mushrooms and
        cider 30

Navarin de mouton 37
New Year menu 85
Nuts 7

Obbie's salad 56
Oils 7
Old English casserole of beef 40
Olives, duckling with 46
Onion:
    French onion soup 20
Orange:
    Fresh orange jelly 69
    Oranges with liqueur and
        praline 81
    Pancakes St Clements 70
    Porc à l'orange 36

Pancakes:
    Pancake batter 62
    Pancakes St Clements 70
Paprika chicken 49
Parsley jelly, ham in 92
Pasta 7
Pastry:
    Easy mix pastry with oil 62
    Shortcrust pastry 62
Peach:
    Peach and ginger salad 57
    Peaches in brandy 69
Peppers, stuffed green 17
Pheasant:
    Faisan en casserole 85
Pies:
    Fish pie 33
    Lemon and chicken pie 93

Pilaf of rice 53
Pineapple:
    Rice pilaf 53
Pizza quiche 14
Plaice with mushrooms and
    cider 30
Polly's lapin à la moutarde 48
Polyunsaturated fats 7
Pork:
    Porc à l'orange 36
    Porc aux pruneaux 36
Portuguese cod 28
Potato:
    Riced potatoes 54
Poultry and game 44–9. *See also*
    Chicken etc.
Praline 81
Prune:
    Porc aux pruneaux 36
Psari plaki 29
Pudding:
    Rich and light Christmas
        pudding 84
Pulses 7
Pumpkin:
    Italian leek and pumpkin soup
        80

Quiches:
    Hazelnut and leek quiche 17
    Pizza quiche 14
    Spinach quiche 16

Rabbit:
    Polly's lapin à la moutarde 48
Ratatouille 54
Rating system 8
Red cabbage 52
Redcurrant:
    Flamri de semoule 72
Rhubarb, compote of 68
Rice 7:
    Kedgeree 32
    Rice pilaf 53
    Rice salad 57
Riced potatoes 54
Roast beef fillet 41
Roast chicken with tarragon 46
Roast lamb 36
Roast turkey, traditional 82

Salad:
    Avocado pear salad 57
    Carrot salad 56
    Chicken, celery and walnut
        salad 90
    Coleslaw 56
    Obbie's salad 56

Peach and ginger salad 57
Rice salad 57
Salmon:
    Cold salmon 89
    Gravad lax 16
    Salmon mousse 92
    Salmon parcels 32
    Smoked salmon 12
Saltimbocca 37
Saturated fat 6
Sauces:
    Béchamel sauce 61
    Brandy butter 65
    Cranberry sauce 61
    Cucumber and mint sauce 64
    Cucumber sauce 65
    Cumberland sauce 60
    French dressing 60
    Garlic and tarragon sauce 29
    Horseradish sauce 40
    Mayonnaise 60
    Sauce diable 81
    Tomato sauce 61
    Velouté sauce 61
Shortcrust pastry 62
Smoked fish starters 12
Soufflé:
    Apricot soufflé 73
Soups 19–25:
    Artichoke soup 21
    Carrot and tomato soup 25
    Country vegetable soup 25
    Courgette and cucumber soup
        22
    French onion soup 20
    Fresh tomato soup 21
    Gazpacho 22
    Iced cucumber soup 24
    Italian leek and pumpkin soup
        80
    Spinach soup 21
    Vichyssoise 24
    Walnut soup 20
    Winter vegetable soup 20
Soured cream, low cholesterol
    65
Spaghetti alla marinara 38
Special occasions, menus for
    78–85
Spinach:
    Spinach quiche 16
    Spinach soup 21
Starters:
    Avocado and caviar mousse 14
    Fresh tomato juice cocktail 13
    Gravad lax 16
    Hazelnut and leek quiche 17
    Melon with Vermouth 13
    Mushrooms en cocotte 12

Pizza quiche 14
Smoked fish starters 12
Spinach quiche 16
Stuffed green peppers 17
Tagliatelle romana 14
Tomates farcies duxelles 12
Stuffed green peppers 17
Stuffed pot-roasted chicken 45

Tagliatelle romana 14
Tarragon:
    Chicken with white wine and
        tarragon 44
    Garlic and tarragon sauce for
        steamed fish 29
    Roast chicken with tarragon 46
Tomato:
    Carrot and tomato soup 25
    Fresh tomato juice cocktail 13
    Fresh tomato soup 21
    Tomates farcies duxelles 12
    Tomato sauce 61
Topinambours provençale 53
Trout:
    Smoked trout 12
    Trout with almonds 30
Tuiles d'amandes 77
Turkey:
    Traditional roast turkey 82
    Turkey in Vermouth 49

Veal:
    Italian veal casserole 38
    Saltimbocca 37
Vegetables 7. *See also* Artichoke
    etc.
    Country vegetable soup 25
    Ratatouille 54
    Winter vegetable soup 20
Velouté sauce 61
Vermouth, melon with 13
Vermouth, turkey in 49
Vichyssoise 24

Walnut:
    Chicken, celery and walnut
        salad 90
    Walnut soup 20
Which foods to eat 9
Winter vegetable soup 20

Yogurt:
    Apricot yogurt 68
    Homemade yogurt 64
    Mackerel with yogurt and
        chives 29